Gamaliel Bradford

Types of American character

Gamaliel Bradford

Types of American character

ISBN/EAN: 9783743333062

Manufactured in Europe, USA, Canada, Australia, Japa

Cover: Foto ©Suzi / pixelio.de

Manufactured and distributed by brebook publishing software
(www.brebook.com)

Gamaliel Bradford

Types of American character

TYPES

OF

AMERICAN CHARACTER

BY

GAMALIEL BRADFORD, Jr.

New York

MACMILLAN AND COMPANY

AND LONDON

1895

Norwood Press

J. S. Cushing & Co. — Berwick & Smith

Norwood Mass. U.S.A.

PREFACE.

It is not pretended that the sketches of character contained in this little volume present more than a few phases of American life, and those not the most prominent. That life, so new in its conditions, so varied and rich and full of interest, offers an inexhaustible field of study to the critical observer, and anything like an adequate presentation of it would require a wider acquaintance with men and things than I can ever hope to lay claim to. I have simply studied a type here and there as they came within my reach.

The American Pessimist and The
American Epicurean are certainly not
to be met with every day. The American Idealist is perhaps somewhat local,
at least as I have sketched him. The
American Man of Letters deals rather
with the conditions of a literary life
than with a literary man. The American Philanthropist alone is a type at
once widely represented and distinctly
American.

In treating these subjects I have
unavoidably been brought in contact
with the most far-reaching philosophical problems. Whether it is possible
to deduce consistent opinions in regard
to these problems from anything I have
said, I do not know ; but if the reader
succeeds in accomplishing this, he will
do more than I can do myself. My

wish is rather to suggest and stimulate than to conclude : in the present state of science and philosophy it seems to me the more useful function.

I am afraid that some of the essays breathe a spirit of gloom and melancholy. This I am sorry for ; for I have come to feel that the two things most desirable and most to be cultivated in this world are love and joy, and I believe that it is possible to cultivate these things far more than we now do.

CONTENTS.

ix

Of the Essays contained in this volume, three, "The American Pessimist," "The American Idealist," and "The American Out of Doors," have appeared in the *Atlantic Monthly* and are reprinted with the permission of Messrs. Houghton, Mifflin & Co. The others are now printed for the first time.

.

TYPES OF
AMERICAN CHARACTER.

---◆---

THE AMERICAN PESSIMIST.

PESSIMISM is a philosophy greatly in repute just now. Schopenhauer and Hartmann are in the mouths of many people who have not read their works at all, and of some who have read them with very little understanding. Many people who call themselves pessimists, however, hardly go the full length, or are conscious what they are proclaiming. To believe deliberately that the whole universe exists for nothing but evil, misery, and suffering ; that there is a power, or an unconscious force, which finds a pleasure, or follows a natural tendency, in the mere causing of destruction, is to believe something very contrary to the natural inclinations of humanity. For this is more, far more, than simple materialism ; more than the mere belief that nature is a vast, inexorable machine, indifferent to the welfare of the sentient world. Materialism is consistent with a philosophy of great calmness and resignation, if not of joy. But to be a pessimist philosophically is to feel one's self in fierce and deadly antagonism with the universe, to hate with redoubled hatred all that is manifestly pernicious, and to see in all that is apparently alluring nothing but the hollow magic of a snare.

Nor is it easy to think that pessimism has ever been a prevalent system of philosophy, or indeed, until to-day, an

elaborated system of philosophy at all,
at least among Western peoples, and
outside of some vast and shadowy
dream-vision of Asia. A theory so
enervating could not have flourished
among the pushing and practical races
of Europe : it is too inconsistent with
all action, too blighting to force and
vitality of will. But pessimism as a
mood, not as a system, is as old as
the world, and as lasting as the thinking animal itself. We are all optimists
and pessimists by turns. We all have
our after-dinner dreams, when life is
suffused with a glow of rose. We all
have our moments of dejection and
despair, caused perhaps at times by
some great grief, but full as often the
result of a little over-fatigue, a jarring
of the nerves, an indigestion, and we
become temporarily as black pessimists as Leopardi.

Yes, it is coeval with the birth of thought itself, the wild and sobbing shriek of overburdened grief, the cold sigh of indifference and *ennui*. We hear it in Job with a burst of passion: "Man that is born of a woman is of few days, and full of trouble. He cometh forth like a flower, and is cut down: he fleeth also as a shadow, and continueth not." We hear it in the terrible verdict of Ecclesiastes: "For who knoweth what is good for man in this life, all the days of his vain life which he spendeth as a shadow? for who can tell a man what shall be after him under the sun?" Lucretius overflows with it: —

"Surgit amari aliquid medio de fonte leporum."

Nor is this tone less familiar to the Christian than to the antique mind. Religious writers often dwell on the misery of this world to bring out the attractions of the next, but the misery of this seems the prominent feature.

Nor is the cry of agony confined to dark and melancholy souls. It is more frequent with them, but the great master spirits of the world give way at times. Even Shakspere, bright magician, skilled in loveliness and charm, had his moments of despair, — moments unknown to us except for the sonnets: —

"Tired with all these, for restful death I cry."

Even Emerson, most optimistic of men, has touches here and there, if one looks for them, of vast discouragement.

When the warm autumn evenings settle down, who can resist this mood; or in the first days of bursting spring, when the world is flooded, drenched, with vitality, and one asks one's self in terror, almost, For what is it all, for what, for what? — so resistless is the flow and tide of nature, so aimless and incomprehensible, so vast. The frail intelligence of man seems diluted in this wider element of semi-nothingness, of unprecipitated being. Again, on some clear October or January morning, it is as if the will of the universe were concentrated in the muscles of one's own right arm. Strange uncontrollable shifting of our moods and purposes!

But there is a pessimism which is a matter neither of mood nor of theory, but of temperament. Most men are born with a moderate view, taking things as they come, but some with a natural tendency to see the world all white or all black. Who does not know the constitutional optimist, who

is always well, always has been well,
or always is going to be well; who is
pleased with the present, satisfied with
the past, full of gorgeous hope for the
future; for whom it never rains, or
shines, or blows, except for the benefit
of some one; who sees what he calls
the good side in all events, in all
people; who makes one wish, sometimes, that some misfortune would
befall him signal enough to make him
"curse God and die"? Who does
not know the constitutional pessimist,
to whom the opposite of this description applies; who may not have intelligence or knowledge enough to accept
the theories of Schopenhauer and Leopardi, but who carries them out in
practice? Every inauspicious glance
of Nature is especially for him. The
dust flies for him, the frost bites for
him, the whole planetary system re-

volves with the sole end of frustrating
his purposes. One wearies, at times,
of the optimist, but, except for those
who are obliged to tolerate him, a prolonged cohabitation with such a pessimist becomes simply intolerable.

This is but a crude form of constitutional pessimism, however, — a form
of indigestion, perhaps I should
rather say, peculiarly attendant on
the combination of a vigorous temperament with a lack of occupation.
There is another manifestation of the
tendency, infinitely finer and more
subtle, — the only one, as I think,
really worthy of the name. This spe-
cies of pessimism is found, I suppose,
all over the world; most intellectual
maladies are, though this may never
have been so highly developed as in
our nineteenth century. But it has
especially come under my observation

here in our own America; and it is as
it exists here that I wish to describe
it. Not that it is very common.
Many of my readers will say they do
not know such a person as I am por-
traying; but some will be able to lay
their fingers on one instantly. The
disease, too, is important, not from
its quantity, but from its quality; it
attacks some of the very clearest and
richest and subtlest minds among us.

This pessimism is wholly different
from the crude discontent and lack of
harmony with surroundings that I have
referred to above. Such a man as we
are speaking of has too much philosophy, if I may call it so, too much
pride, too large a view, to set himself
in a pitiful and petty antagonism with
the ample and eternal forces which go
to make up what we call Nature. He
has a suave indifference to small dis-

comforts that at times leads superficial people to confound him with the optimist; for he has few of those turbulent and fleeting bursts of temper which overcome the serenest of us. He faces great misfortunes and even small annoyances with the same inexplicable, unalterable smile, — a smile more fitted to move the looker-on to tears than to any outbreak of accordant mirth.

No, the modern pessimist, the true, incurable pessimist, is not, perhaps, a pessimist at all. He does not rail, or curse God, or despise man. If his state of mind can be described, it is by saying that he has thought, not himself, but everything besides himself, into a shadow. He is a man who has embarked on the wide sea of intellectual discovery, and has found that for him it is a barren sea, blank, desolate, — a sea shoreless, where the traveller voyages on aimlessly forever in a misty void.] He is a man for whom the fevered, passionate whirl of life, so fierce, so intense, so real, to other men, is but a disordered dream, — a dream of which no one knows the beginning, and no one can prophesy the end. He is a man to whom the present is a reality only in comparison with the utter darkness of the future and the past, — a man to whom faith and hope are shadows, and charity is the emptiest and vainest of super-structures, from which all foundation has been eaten away.]

But, some one says, this is not pessimism. You are misusing the word, and disguising in flowery rhetoric something which should go by another name. But no other name will quite cover what I mean. Practical Epicureanism is a philosophy very popular among us, as indeed it has been popular at all times and everywhere, though not always so openly proclaimed and without veil as it is to-day. The practical Epicurean is quite as much without belief as the pessimist I speak of; he is quite as free from prejudices as to morals or religion, quite as ready to disclaim adherence to inherited ideas. But he simply flings all these things aside. From his want of belief, when he reasons at all, he draws a solid and comfortable conclusion: Let us eat, drink, and be merry, for to-morrow we die. That conclusion is the basis, conscious or unconscious, of a vast deal of American life to-day, modified only by the fact that the American has not yet really learned how to enjoy himself, and seeks distraction in endless and feverish mental excitement rather than in the subtle and judiciously husbanded pleasures of the senses.

Now, the life of our pessimist is as far from this as possible. (It is true that he has lost all faith, if he ever had any. He has long ago recognized that the intellect is a will-o'-the-wisp, kindling its fitful gleam, now here, now there, in the vast plashy meadow of perceptive existence, but leading to no sure and solid foothold, drawing the weary wanderer only deeper and deeper in the mire. Yet, knowing this, he cannot resist the fatal charm. He has tasted the alluring sweets of abstract reverie, and he can never give them up. Once caught in the toil of that enchantress, there is no escape, — she, the true Circe, who, instead of enslaving men to the joys of sense, turns those joys themselves into the shadow of a shade. Yes, even if the pessimist would shut up the cavern of his mind and strew it over with the roses and the charm of life, he cannot. Still, still he is haunted with the consciousness of the drear abyss beneath. It is true to him, too true, that tomorrow we die, and, in the face of that fact, how can he eat, drink, and be merry?

But am I not describing an agnostic? To a certain extent, yes. The pessimist, in this sense, does deny the possibility of real knowledge, cognition of the Absolute, as does the agnostic. Yet no! He does not deny or assert anything. He himself knows nothing about the Absolute, but others may. After all, the agnostic belongs to a sect, a dogmatic sect, a sect ready for the most part to decry what it calls the superstitions of other people. Now, to our pessimist, dogmatism is, of all things, hateful. Just because he believes nothing, he is alive to the possibility of believing anything or everything. The most monstrous superstition, except as it involves intolerance and cruelty, is to him as worthy of respect as the refined abstractions of the Hegelian. As faiths, they mean to him nothing; as phenomena of the human intelligence, they are alike curious objects for the ceaseless play of thought.

It is true that we might fall back on the term "sceptic." But that, also, implies a system, bears with it some inference of Pyrrhonism, and a hardened determination to question everything whatever. So natural are theory and a creed to humanity that it erects even its profoundest doubt into a dogma.

Therefore, until something better is

suggested, we still must call the subject of our examination a pessimist.
He is not a shrieking fanatic, like
Leopardi or Schopenhauer, who parades his own despair in the eyes of
an unsympathetic world. Such dem-
onstrations seem to him crude and
unwarrantable. The deepest mystery
of things is too august to be hailed
with such abuse as a fretful child
showers upon its nurse. But his pessimism is rather an indefinable shade
of gray which pervades his whole view
of life, — silent, uncomplaining, but
profoundly hopeless.

It is here that the peculiarity of the
American type must be taken into
account. Men such as I have been
describing are to be found all over
Europe, all over the civilized world.
In France they are very numerous,
and the great French literature of to-

day is largely built up by them.   Indeed, the tradition of the race began
long ago in France, in more or less
disguised forms; clad in gorgeous
rhetoric in Chateaubriand, touched
with fevered passion in Sénancour,
nursed to his own destruction by
Maurice de Guérin.   It is the ground
tone of the great French realistic
novelists, Stendhal, Balzac, Flaubert,
the De Goncourts, Zola, the half-
French Turgeneff; and, in the younger
generation, of such men as Paul Bour-
get and Guy de Maupassant.   But
there is an immense distinction between these men and their American fellow.   He is as profoundly and
completely sceptical as they are; but,
owing to a difference of race, or, it
may be, to the traditions of Puritan-
ism that still linger in his blood, he
is less brutal than they, — is, in fact,

c

as far as possible from brutality. From their complete disbelief in all moral law, they deduce a profound viciousness and uncleanness of tone and habit, not from any great pleasure in the enjoyments of the senses, but simply from hatred of the conventional, the *bourgeois*. To him such licentiousness is wholly repulsive, it offends his taste; he lives and thinks as purely as a fanatic.

Yes, he has inherited many things from his Puritan ancestors, this child of the nineteenth century, whom they would spurn and scorn more even than the fiercest heretic or the most godless debauchee. Their glowing love of a saintly ideal still lingers in his veins, possesses him at times with a wild desire for the beauty of holiness, making the void only blacker and bleaker when it fades away. He has inherited

from them a fastidious scrupulosity
of conscience, which haunts him in
minute details, even when conscience
itself has become to him an idle illusion. Vices he has none. Faults he
may have, arising from indifference
and lack of enthusiasm; but the more
passive virtues, gentleness, tenderness,
mildness, infinite toleration, — no one
has them more than he.   These things
make him beloved in spite of the chill
which he casts over everything, for he
is ready to listen to other people's joys
and woes, and not burden them with
his own.   Indeed, simply to meet him
and talk with him, you would never
become aware of the profound darkness at the bottom of his heart.   You
would think him ready to agree with
your own Methodism, or Episcopalian-
ism, or what not.   Only rarely, if you
are unusually penetrating, there would

be a glance that would put you on your guard.

Is he then hypocritical, inconsistent? Inconsistent, yes. I have heard a Philistine described as one "who lives from convention, not from conviction." If the definition is accurate, our pessimist is a thorough Philistine; for he abhors convictions, and has none of any kind whatever. Yet the poor man must live.

And he does live. If you ask him, he will probably say that life brings him, on the whole, more misery than happiness, by far. Yet he lives, either because he is mistaken, or because the tremendous unreasoning instinct that makes us cry out for life — life, good or bad — predominates over him as over the rest of us. He lives, often, to a gray old age, and sees his children around him. There are bright spots,

too, even for him, sunny nooks in an
autumn day, where he can fly the cold
north and dream that there is something that is not a dream; something
stable, worth grasping, worth loving;
something that will not fade away.
But, for the rest, he bears his lot as
he can, without murmur or complaint;
looking on at the vast and varied ban-
quet of the world, from which he alone
goes away unsatisfied; gazing, an idle
and yet not an uninterested spectator,
at the curious and futile show which
the vagaries of language and the traditions of our ancestors have taught
us to call life.

THE AMERICAN IDEALIST.

THE word "idealism" is in many minds connected with a philosophical system that is mainly negative. The critical and destructive portion of Kant's work has become so widely known as the basis of German philosophy that an idealist is supposed to be one who believes the whole empirical world to be a delusion; who sees no reality but his own thought, and cannot rest even that reality on a solid foundation; a nihilist, in short. Could anything be more mistaken? Is there a philosophy more triumphant, more overflowing with faith, more world-storming, than true ideal-

ism? Is there a man whose convictions are firmer, more self-asserting,
more vigorous, more joyous, than
those of the true idealist? Instead of
doubting the existence of things, he
is penetrated with the intensity, the
self-demonstrating sureness, of reality;
he cannot resist it if he would; every
moment of life is to him crowded and
packed with certainty, though perhaps
not so much with the certainty of
material phenomena as with that of
moral and spiritual facts, of *ideas.*
He is by nature a believer. Everything shows, I think, that Kant
himself, in spite of his "world-over-
turning" speculations, was the profoundest of believers.

At the same time something can be
said for the common view. If the
idealist does not dissolve the world in
his own mind, he projects his own

mind upon the world. He lives among theories, among types, to which facts must accommodate themselves or suffer for it. He does not love inductive methods, prefers working *a priori*. How can things be except as they ought to be? Every idealist constructs in his own way a skeleton like the great logical schemes of Plato or Hegel, round which the world of perception must flow gently, and shape itself in a fleshly garment, sometimes beautifully draped and adjusted, sometimes falling in harsh folds with a melancholy stiffness. In this sense it may be said that the idealist destroys the world, and builds it for himself anew.

The division on these lines into idealist and realist absorbs all humanity. There are the men who see things as they are and the men who see them as they would have them. To put it more fairly, there are those who take each fact of experience by itself, letting it get connected with other facts as it can; there are those who find for every fact its proper place in the vast and perfect order of nature. These two different classes can never quite understand each other or work together. In one the subjective is subordinated to the objective; in the other the subject rides triumphant and supreme, the object being reduced to servile insignificance.

The scientific tone of mind, the modern critical spirit, is distinctly realist. It aims to make itself a mere passive instrument, played upon, like an Æolian harp, by all the influences of the outer world. Indeed, the intellect pure and simple does not favour idealism, which springs essentially from the moral side of our nature. The intellect is always striving to be impersonal; the heart, the emotions, are what drive us, with feverish intensity, to assert ourselves. Now, the intellect has become more predominant in the nineteenth century than it has ever been before in the history of the world.

Yet what a curious illustration of nature's revenges is the spread of pessimism side by side with this mighty development of the intellect! Pessimism is idealism turned inside out. Every pessimist has in him the elements of an enthusiastic idealist; for if he did not imagine a more perfect world, why should he find so much fault with this? Only the clear-eyed intellect thinks the ideal world hopelessly far away; and the dull, muddy world about us seems vile in compari-

son. A French critic remarks: "I
wrote it twenty-five years ago, 'the
supernatural'"—let us read, the ideal,
—"'is the sphere of the soul,' and I
see no reason for changing my mind.
The only thing I would add now is
this melancholy reflection, that one
may demand the Absolute without
being sure of getting it. The child,
also, cries for the moon, when it has
seen the reflection in a well."

Of the numerous spiritual types that
humanity presents, some are perma-
nent and some are transitory. A good
example of the latter is the miser.
There is plenty of meanness, of nig-
gardliness and foolish sparing, in the
nineteenth century; but you do not
often find, in this country, at any rate,
a man who hoards gold simply for the
pleasure of counting it, of eyeing it,
—who grudges equally the spending

of one dollar and of a thousand. People seek to acquire money, as they have always done, because money gives the means for gratifying their passions, because it gives power; but they do not often seek it for the actual accumulation of precious metal. This may be owing to the colossal size of modern fortunes, which makes money less a reality than a dream; it is more probably caused by the introduction of paper currency and the banking system. The clink of gold affords a pleasure not to be found in fingering greenbacks. Certain literary figures have lost their interest for us on account of this change, — figures like Molière's Harpagon and the heroes of many of La Fontaine's fables.

On the other hand, some types belong to this century only, or to this and the preceding. The philanthro-

pist is one of these, — the man who
devotes his life to working for mankind not from any lofty religious principle, sometimes even with no great
belief in the goodness or worth of
humanity; doing it either from pure
sympathy and love, or because he has
no other means of satisfying a restless
desire for action.   Another modern
type is the critic, perhaps I should
say the scientist, who has reduced his
own personality to a minimum, and
lives on curiosity; who thrusts himself into the spiritual garments of
other men, or probes the secrets of
nature, drawing into his own veins
the blood and life that circulate elsewhere.

But idealists are confined neither to
the ninth century nor to the nineteenth.   The first man who framed for
himself another life beyond this world

or outside of it, the first man who laboured and toiled with hand and brain to bring about a paradise in the future, or dreamed of a paradise in the past, was the first idealist. In spite of all negations, of all iconoclasms, of the downfall of this creed and of that creed, the world will never see the last. The ideal is infinite in its persistence, infinite in its protean power of reëmbodiment, remanifestation. All it demands is faith in something, belief in something, beyond the passing sensuous impression: give it that, and it will conquer the world. For its advantage over positivism and scepticism consists in its being affirmative, in its perpetual self-assertion. Those who follow it follow undoubting, absolutely mastered. In Heine's words, — and let me remark that Heine wrote " Idea," and not " ideas,"

as it stands in the epigraph of one of
our magazines: "We do not seize upon
the Idea; the Idea seizes us, and en-
slaves us, and lashes us into the arena,
where we fight for it like gladiators,
whether we will or no." What a mas-
querade this worship of the Idea gives
us, sweeping down in bright order
through the shadowy past! The ob-
stinate hope of the Jews for their Mes-
siah, the patriotism of the Greeks at
Thermopylæ, the Christian martyrs,
the glittering Crusades, the Renaissance, the sanguinary passion of the
French Revolution, — these are the
gleaming points in the great web of
enthusiasm for all causes and all faiths.
Believe! Believe! Only believe! And
all things shall be added unto you.

It will be seen from the above enu-
meration that nations are idealists as
well as individuals. Is not the Bible

the monument of indomitable idealism
in a whole race? — a race narrow,
indeed, in its conceptions, not much
concerned with the intellectual problems that please the Aryans, yet in-
tensely and fiercely moral, and showing
its idealism in the positive force of its
morality, in not being content with
perfecting itself, but in being deter-
mined to overcome the whole world.
Has idealism ever been manifested
with more energy and splendour than
in the lament of Job, or the denuncia-
tion of David, or the lovely visions
of Isaiah? "For, behold, I create
new heavens and a new earth: and the
former shall not be remembered, nor
come into mind." Is not that the
text of the idealist everywhere? "But
unto you that fear my name shall the
Sun of righteousness arise with healing
in his wings." For that rising not

only Jew but Gentile waits, has waited, and will wait forever, with the fervour of an unconquerable hope.

A blind enthusiasm of the same sort, though grosser in its materialism, was at the bottom of the great Mohamme- dan movement. The intenser form of idealism, at least in religious matters, seems to be found outside the Aryan races, which agrees with what I said above as to the results of intellectual development in individuals. Even among Aryan nations, however, there are, as one can see, vast differences in this respect. Perhaps, taking into account the fact that we must live in this world as it is, with all its imper- fections, the Greeks, in their best days, came as near to a just harmo- nizing of the real and the ideal as is possible. The Romans, on the other hand, were, as a people, positivists

D

beyond any the world has seen; positivists to such a point that, with the
exception of two great poems, — even
those largely imitative, — they alone
of all important nations, ancient or
modern, left behind them no trace of
original work in any one of the fine
arts.

Among modern European nations,
the English are most like the Romans,
in this as in other things. Their
poetry saves them from the same degree of reproach; yet their poetry is at
its best in the drama, and the drama
is the form of poetry that lends itself
least to idealistic purposes. The
French are more distinctly idealist.
Indeed, we may safely say that, generally speaking, the Kelts always are
so, while the Teutonic races are
soberer, more practical. A moment's
consideration of English history and

character compared with French or Irish will suffice to prove this.

To return to individuals. This enthusiasm, faith, takes naturally very different forms in different minds. In some it is calm, serene, gentle; works upon mankind by mild and sweet persuasiveness, by an influence that spreads unconsciously, yet all the more powerfully. In others it is stormy, impetuous, rejoicing in difficulties, rejoicing in struggle and sacrifice, seeming to acquire firmer conviction by the sense of victory hardly earned. We need not go far for examples of both these classes. Where could we find the contrast better illustrated than in the Founder of Christianity and its greatest apostle? Paul cries, not once, but again and again, in varying words: "For I delight in the law of God after the inward man: but I see another law in my members, warring against the law of my mind, and bringing me into captivity to the law of sin which is in my members. O wretched man that I am! who shall deliver me from the body of this death?" How different, ah, how different is this other tone! "Take my yoke upon you, and learn of me. . . . For my yoke is easy, and my burden is light."

Examples of such opposite tendencies might be multiplied infinitely. In literature, take, for instance, Byron and Shelley. Byron was certainly an idealist in his way; but he would have been inclined to mend the world by shattering it to pieces. Shelley, whose "passion for reforming the world" marks him as one of the most intense idealists of our century, was the sweetest of men.

It is clear enough that the idealist
is not necessarily either moral or religious. What he must have is an
abiding and inspiring enthusiasm for
something that demands devotion and
sacrifice; this something may be religion, it may be humanity, it may be
beauty, it may be one's country, it
may be power, it may be wealth. The
distinction lies not so much in the
object as in the spirit with which it is
pursued. Alexander was an idealist;
Cæsar was not. Shakspere, so far as
we can judge, was not; Milton was.
Napoleon, in spite of his hatred of
idéologues, was an idealist himself.
There is no way to make this felt more
clearly than by contrasting him with
Wellington, in whom the genius of his
country may be said to have been embodied, as, in a certain sense, that of
France was in Napoleon. The ideal-

ist may, then, be selfish in as high a degree, as absolutely, as he may be virtuous. Indeed, even when his preoccupation is wholly with what is high and pure, he may be caustic, crabbed, unlovable, to those about him. He often is so, with his impatience at not being understood, his keen perception of the woful difference between the world as it is and the world as he would have it.

This is the limitation, the negative side. Conviction, in this world, so often brings intolerance. The French writer I quoted just now says elsewhere: "The fundamental dogma of intolerance is that there are dogmas; that of tolerance, that there are only opinions." But the Idea is more than a dogma, it is a fact, in the mind of the believer. How can he look upon it as a mere opinion, discutable, dis-

putable? How can he put himself in
the place of another, disown his own
position, admit even the possibility of
being wrong? He works by sight, not
by faith; by an intuition that allows
no question and no doubt. Hence
the sweetest of idealists must think
you ignorant and to be pitied, if you
differ from him. He will not abuse
or revile you, but he will regard you
at best as an object for conversion.
The idealist who is not sweet will not
refrain from expressing his opinion.

To come to what is properly American. The typical American is, or
was, English in his origin, and I have
said that the English are not idealists.
Furthermore, it was the Puritans who
emigrated to this country, and the
Puritans embodied what was least
idealistic in the English nature. It
is bold, perhaps, to say so, but I am

convinced that what makes the Puritans unattractive, in spite of their virtues, is this very fact, that they were
not idealists. For the most part, the
English religious movement of the
seventeenth century was a revolt of
common sense, as indeed was the
Reformation in general. The English
political movement of the seventeenth
century was of the same nature, as
one may see by contrasting it with
the French Revolution, Hampden
with Robespierre. It may be said
that if this be the case the English
were blessed in not being idealists.
With that we have nothing to do in
this simple search after facts. What
I have asserted above is exactly what
Matthew Arnold meant when he spoke
of Luther as the " Philistine of genius
in religion," Bunyan as the "Philistine of genius in literature," Crom-

well as the "Philistine of genius in
politics," all taken from the group
of men connected with new-born
Protestantism.

The Puritans who left England for
America were perhaps more idealistic
than those who remained at home;
yet the most striking thing about the
founders of New England is their
stern good sense. It has stuck by
their descendants till the present day.
The characteristic religion of New
England, Unitarianism, is the religion of good sense, the least idealistic
religion that has ever professed to
connect itself with Christianity.

The American of to-day, however,
either from race intermixture or from
influences of climate or of institutions, is manifestly different from his
English progenitor. He is quicker,
keener, less conservative, though still

conservative. His intelligence is in-
ventive, and proverbially seeks rapid
ways to come at things. He is extremely practical, — more than that,
material; dazed, it would seem, by
the immense resources of his country, by the immense opportunities it
affords for accumulating wealth, and
with it power. He is, for the present, wholly absorbed in the means;
careless of the end, if there be an end
at all. Yet his spiritual eye is shut
rather than blinded. If you can open
it, it is wonderfully quick and penetrating. He is restless, too, dissatisfied with traditions, with old-world
beliefs, doctrines, ideas. He half
thinks there should be a new religion, as vast and modern as his needs.
We perceive the same restlessness in
the later Roman world, with somewhat similar conditions. Men were

dissatisfied with their old faith; all vital belief in it had disappeared; everywhere they were doubting, wondering.
Before the spread of Christianity, all
sorts of religions from the East —
Mithraism, for instance — found numerous followers. In such a soil
Christianity could not but grow vigor-
ously. The Roman world resembled
us, indeed, only in the sudden increase of material prosperity. The
newness of conditions is far more
general with us than it was with them.
Yet here, too, what a hold has been
taken by Spiritualism, by Christian
Science, by the mystical philosophies
of India, even where they are only
half, if at all, understood!

When the American is possessed
by the Idea, he is possessed by it
thoroughly; not with a Celtic unrea-
son, but with an enthusiasm that

seems quite out of harmony with his
ordinary half-sceptical self, and that
goes great lengths. The most interesting point in the history of American thought is the transcendental
movement of the first half of this century, which was idealism incarnate.
Practically, it showed itself in that
curious experiment, Brook Farm,
which was an attempt to realize what
has been in one form or another the
social Utopia of all idealists; an
attempt to overcome the biting stress
of individualism, to "pool," as the
railroad men say, the interests of all
humanity; an attempt — which failed.
What was far more serious, and what
did not fail, was the great antislavery
movement, as truly a result of idealism here as was the French Revolution in Europe, and managed in a far
purer spirit. It has been argued, to

be sure, that the English got rid of slavery with less idealism, but without bloodshed. The cases were, however, very different.

The list of great names connected with all these movements is not a short one. Active in the antislavery agitation, we have Garrison, Phillips, Sumner. More especially connected with transcendentalism, we have the group that centred in Concord: Alcott, about whom critical judgments differ most; Margaret Fuller, pathetic in her actual fate without any addition of romance; Thoreau, robust, self-asserting, not to say egotistical, — more arrogant than some of his comrades, but touched with a fine and peculiar genius most nearly allied to the greatest of them all. Lastly, rising with his whole figure above these, who are only grouped about the pedes-

tal upon which he stands, comes the
representative American idealist, —
one may almost say the representative
idealist of all times and nations; the
man who came nearest to uniting the
high enthusiasm of the saint with
the calm vision of the seer, who
touched with a holy fire the speculations of Plato and Hegel, who blended
the philosophy of Germany with the
mysticism of Asia; the man who, for
the first time in nineteen centuries,
owned the all-importance of religion,
and yet looked forward, and not back,
— Ralph Waldo Emerson. No doubt
the Puritan lack of imagination does
make itself felt in Emerson, at times
almost repulsively; no doubt minds
of another type do and must weary of
his eternal optimism; but never was
there a truer servant of the Idea than
he; never has the high enthusiasm of

that service been better voiced than it so often was by him.

"The soul is not a compensation, but a life. The soul is. Under all this running sea of circumstance, whose waters ebb and flow with perfect balance, lies the aboriginal abyss of real Being. . . . Nothing, Falsehood, may indeed stand as the great night or shade on which, as a background, the living universe paints itself forth, but no fact is begotten by it; it cannot work, for it is not; it cannot work any harm; it cannot work any good. It is harm inasmuch as it is worse not to be than to be.

"In a virtuous action I properly am; in a virtuous act I add to the world; I plant into deserts conquered from Chaos and Nothing, and see the darkness receding on the limits of the horizon. There can be no excess to

love, none to knowledge, none to
beauty, when these attributes are considered in the purest sense. The soul
refuses limits, and always affirms an
optimism, never a pessimism."

Essay after essay is but one con-
tinuous joyous proclamation of the
permanence, the inexhaustible vitality, of the Idea.

As was natural, this vigorous and
potent personality influenced a great
number of people. Many of them
sought an expression for their enthusiasm in literature, — some successfully, the majority not so. But there
were others who were contented to
live quietly in the calm and pure
light of their high faith, making no
attempt to communicate it, unless
indirectly by a certain spiritual atmosphere that constantly surrounded
them. One such I have in mind: a

man who was for many years, for life
almost, an intimate friend of Emerson's; who had imbibed his spirit
thoroughly, yet united with it a peculiar gentleness and sweetness all his
own. His nature was feminine in
its delicacy, subtly sensitive to all
impressions, — morbid in some ways,
unquestionably. He was at times the
slave of a conscientiousness that ruled
him tyrannically, exposing him to ridicule from those who did not understand; but the fine purity of his
character, his imaginative sympathy,
his infinite patience, tolerance, readiness to find excuses even for those he
disapproved of, his loyalty and devotion to the people and the ideas he
loved, above all his supreme unworld-
liness and indomitable conviction of
the truth, — when shall we look upon
his like again?

E

The men of that generation have passed away. Have their enthusiasms vanished with them? I do not believe it. Material prosperity has lured us all more or less from the things of the spirit. The high light of thought and devotion seems obscured by the mist of lower passions, sordid rivalries, eager greed. But, as a people, we are not — as yet we are not — corrupted or decadent. We are ever on the watch for what points upward, full of generous impulses, ready sympathies. Above all, we are hopeful; we look forward. We feel in a manner bound to grow to the great destinies of a great country. All sorts of speculative opinions find a ready acceptance. I have alluded to Christian Science, and the fascination exercised by half-mystical theories about new discoveries in the nature of

mind.   Politically, the idealistic tendency shows itself in the projects
of the Nationalists, the followers of
George and Bellamy.   It shows itself
also in agitations for woman's rights
and objects of that nature.   Indeed,
it may be said, in passing, that the
most typical American idealist is a
woman; idealism, with its merits and
defects, being more natural to women
than to men.

No, from whatever source derived,
whether it be a reflection of Divinity
in the human heart, or a mere figment
of the imagination projected on the
realm of "Chaos and old Night," the
Idea can never die, never lose its influence over mankind, never cease to
be the mainspring of all that is ac-
complished in the world, of all progress, of all virtue, of all happiness.
It clothes itself in many forms.   It

puts on and casts off religions and philosophies like worn and faded garments. All these change, but the Idea remains the same. Something outside, something beyond, something larger than itself, humanity must have to strive for, to hope for. It would be useless to oppose this tendency, even if it were desirable. The pessimist will revile it, cherishing it all the while more than any one else. The critic will find in it an ever-changing and infinitely curious object of study. The wise statesman will seek to guide it and profit by it. But he who is a born idealist himself will see in its vitality its justification. He will bow down with his whole heart and soul in infinite worship before the unchanged, immortal spirit of virtue, loveliness, and truth, which, underneath the shifting illusion of the world, is all that is firm, all that is abiding.

DISTINCTION is the mightiest implement of the wise, and the plaything of the idle. Allow me to amuse myself with it for a moment. An Epicurean is one who enjoys life, who lives, so far as possible, by and for enjoyment, and who at the same time analyzes his pleasure and philosophizes about it after his own fashion. Epicurean and materialist are often confounded; but the materialist is simply absorbed in what is external and material. He does not philosophize about it; he does not even always enjoy it. He may be bound down and tyrannized over by it, so that he hates

it, but cannot escape from it, like some
men of business, or even some philanthropists ; for I have known philanthropic materialists, but never a
philanthropic Epicurean. Nor are Epicureanism and paganism identical.
Here, too, there is the difference of
underlying analysis and thought, which
makes, as it were, the lining of the Epicurean's pleasure, and gives it a sort
of bitter-sweet of its own. He observes
and studies himself even in the midst
of the keenest delight. The pagan, on
the other hand, enjoys without observation or analysis. He has the frank,
free gaiety of the fauns of Rubens, who
pass unremittingly from sleep to laughter, and from laughter to sleep, if, indeed, they sleep at all.

It is a notable, though perhaps not
wholly enviable, title to reputation to
have given one's name to a sect like

this ; and it is to be wished that we
knew something more definite of the
life and doctrines of Epicurus, which
have come to us only through the dis-
torting media of his disciples' writings.
We have, however, every reason to
believe that he was a gentle and tolerant man, which is an excellent thing in
a philosopher, and for my part I am
happy to accept the portrait given us
in Landor's celebrated dialogue, where
we find, indeed, certain amiable weak-
nesses, but altogether outweighed by
attractiveness and charm.

When we pass to Epicurus' greatest
disciple, what a difference ! And how
little we find in the *De Rerum Natura*
those qualities which we associate with
the Master, and still more with the
name *Epicurean* in modern times. Is
it probable that Lucretius ever enjoyed himself in the mild sense in

which the word is used by ordinary mortals? Perhaps he knew the fierce delight of struggling with great mental problems, of toiling up vast slopes of argument from the summit of which, when one has reached it, one beholds nothing but barrenness and death, of moulding and straining a hard language into magical harmonies and long waves of echoing sound. But Epicurean — where is the softness, where the grace, where the roses and the smiles? Lucretius rushes at pleasure, battles with it, crushes it, kills himself in seeking to possess it. Some of us do that to-day, but we are not called Epicureans.

But there is a classical representative of the habits, if not always of the doctrines, of Epicurus, who harmonizes much better with our preconceived ideas on the subject; I mean, of

course, Horace. It is a pity that
Horace is out of fashion just now.
When we read Latin at all, we read
Catullus and Lucretius, which is well.
But perhaps Virgil and Horace will
some day come in again, without the
others going out. No one claims for
Horace the lyrical passion of Catullus;
but he has lyrical qualities of his own,
flawless grace, a perfect hold on his
subject, a style perhaps more subtly
and delicately intellectual than that of
any other writer, unless it be Petrarch.
Above all, he had precisely the Epicurean quality we are speaking of, of
taking all the pleasures of life, great
and small, as they came within his
reach, and at the same time that he
enjoyed them with the keenest zest, of
reflecting on them, classifying them,
appreciating, too, their fleetingness,
and emptiness, and vainness, if only

there were anything better to replace
them. What profound wisdom he has
with what endless tolerance and sympathy ! He does not rant and tear a
passion to tatters, unless, alas, when
hired to write conventional morality
by the powers that be ; and even then
you feel that he sings a little after the
fashion of Dodor in *Trilby*, when enter-
taining his inamorata with psalmodic
selections.

We shall hardly, I imagine, find
much Epicureanism in the Europe of
the Dark and Middle Ages. Materialism and brutal paganism, brutality even
beyond paganism, of course, abound.
We shall see enough of the love of
pleasure, but very little of philosophy ;
unless we imagine to ourselves hidden
away in the dim corner of a mediæval
monastery some friar of orders gray,
who has fled thither as to a quiet

refuge from a turbulent and barbarous
world, who passes his days in reading
the classics, with a flask of red wine
and a flask of white, a pretty niece,
and a gentle smile at the follies and
vagaries of mankind.

When we come to the Renaissance,
on the other hand, we shall find Epicureanism in its fullest flower. Even
here we must distinguish it from
paganism ; for the great characteristic
of the Renaissance is chiefly a wild
rush for the delights of life so long
obscured and hid away. Every one
thrust in for his share, and the common herd then, as always, did not
examine nor inquire into the nature of
its deeds. But the fifteenth and sixteenth centuries were peculiarly a time
when men of intellectual power plunged
into every kind of extravagance and
excess, and then they all, more or less,

in the true meaning of *reflection*, turned
to look back upon themselves.   Chief
among these stands Montaigne.   We
know Montaigne as a sceptic.   It is
the name under which Emerson has
treated him, and doubtless represents
accurately a part of his mental attitude.
But Epicurean suits him better still.
Epicureanism does, indeed, presuppose
a certain amount of theoretical scepticism ; but the typical sceptic, even if
he is not a professional philosopher
like Pyrrho, is surely much more
philosophical than Montaigne.   Scepticism implies constant and consistent
thought, a contact with the great
problems of life, which is too apt to
bring a pale brow and an anxious eye.
The rich, rubicund nature of Montaigne and Horace has nothing more
akin to philosophical scepticism than
a good-natured mistrust of dogmas

whether one's own or other people's, and a fancy for amusing oneself at the fireside by stripping the idols both of cave and market-place down to a bare skeleton of nothing. But that keen observation of human life coupled with an endless delight in it, which is the charm of Horace, reappears in Montaigne, free from any trammels of poetical form, abundant, varied, lighted up with infinite humour, illustrated by boundless learning, now playing wantonly on the surface of common needs, now plunging down into the deep recesses of wayward passions, but always smiling, always serene, always tolerant, always free from conventional prejudice.

The nearest English equivalent of Montaigne is Robert Burton of the *Anatomy of Melancholy*. That wonderful book, bristling with quotation and illustration, is an epitome of the

Renaissance in many ways. At the
same time Burton's description, depic-
tion of the pleasures of life, is not, like
Montaigne's, that of a man who has
touched and tasted ; it is that of a
scholar and something of a pedant,
who eyes the promised land wistfully
from without, who listens eagerly to the
enthusiasm of others, and very much
exaggerates in imagination the possibilities of what he might enjoy, but himself never quite dares enter. Nor is
Burton singular in this. Epicureanism
is not thoroughly to the Anglo-Saxon
taste. The English life may have its
period of brutal and unthinking self-
indulgence, but there comes a moral
reaction from the ever-present Philistine within us, of which the grandest
example is the respectable old age of
Shakspere as a worthy, harmless, re-
vered, and thrifty burgess of Stratford.

In this rapid survey we can touch
only the summits. If we pass over
the seventeenth century with its group
of men of letters, of whom so many,
in France at any rate, deserve the title
of Epicurean, we shall find in the
eighteenth much less tendency in this
direction. Voltaire, though he had no
dislike for the pleasant side of life,
seems too petulant, too narrow, too
dry for the true Epicurean spirit.
Rousseau and those who followed in
his wake were enthusiasts, and there is
no such deadly enemy of enthusiasm
as the Epicurean. You may be a fanatic for good or evil, you may preach
salvation or destruction, you may rave
over optimism or pessimism, and the
Epicurean will smile at you, not with
the bitter mockery of Voltaire, but
with a patronizing expression, as who
should say: " My dear Sir, how soon

all this will boil over into the cool dust of the grave."

At the threshold of the nineteenth century we meet with Goethe, and it would be curious to examine why we can set him down so definitely as un-Epicurean. He is not a Christian, surely, he whom Heine called the great pagan of the century. Yet as surely we cannot call him pagan as we call Ariosto pagan or Boccaccio. Is there, perhaps, after all in Goethe a little touch of the pedant? Or had he, too, his enthusiasm, that of the artist, burning in him as a clear and constant flame, rather than as the devouring fire which ate away the hearts of Flaubert and Leopardi?

But, so far as literature is concerned, we shall find our most interesting examples of the modern Epicurean in contemporary France. Perhaps it would not be wholly fair to apply the name to Sainte-Beuve. If not, it would be because he laboured with an earnestness almost amounting to enthusiasm at the art which he had chosen. Yet his general way of looking at life comes perilously near that of some authors we have been considering, especially when we take into account not only his formal criticism, but his detached thoughts and the record of him that has come to us through his friends. He himself tells us that he arrived at wisdom, not by the road of Spinoza and Hegel, but by that of Solomon and Epicurus, something, I suppose, like the broad-gated way that leadeth to other things besides wisdom. Among the critics who have succeeded Sainte-Beuve we might look even more successfully for men who illustrate precisely what I

F

mean by the modern Epicurean. But
the best example of all is the great
writer whom France has recently lost,
Ernest Renan. If we compare Renan
with Montaigne, we shall get all the
difference between the nineteenth and
the sixteenth century, difference in
manners, difference in traditional morals, difference in intellectual pursuits.
It is quite impossible to imagine Montaigne finding his pleasure in the acquisition of a profound knowledge of
Hebrew, or the study of the Semitic
peoples. It is impossible to imagine
Montaigne in a dusty class-room, lecturing spectacled to a small assembly
of pedantic students, to imagine Montaigne a professor. But down underneath the superficial difference we
come to the Epicurean basis common
to both ; the complete disregard of a
formalized system of philosophy, the

endless delight in the play of humanity
and life, the universal toleration and
indulgence for the enthusiasms and the
follies of others. And it is perfectly
conceivable that if Montaigne had lived
three hundred years later he would
have come to see how merely barbarous were all his pursuits, beside the
exquisite pleasure of baffling the Philistine journalist with touches of irony
finer and subtler than that of Aristophanes or Heine.

Now let us cross the Atlantic in
pursuit of our Epicurean of America.
If we confound Epicureanism with materialism or paganism, we shall find
it scattered broadcast in this beloved
country of ours. I suppose we must
look upon business as one of the forms
of materialism, though naturally one
may engage in it without being ma-
terialized. And if I wished to draw

the most universal and most truly
American type possible, I should begin
with the Man of Business. We see
him everywhere, do we not, and everywhere substantially the same? To be
sure, in Boston, he generally speaks
good English and may be a college
graduate; in the Far West he is apt to
be rough in manner and of cosmopol-
itan extraction; in Chicago he is overflowing with a joyous confidence in the
city of his choice; in the South he has
a certain dignified slowness, a pride of
caste, whatever be his occupation, and a
rooted hatred of " niggers "; and everywhere he has one great tie of common
humanity, — business. See him on a
street-corner waiting for a car, absorbed as Archimedes. Does he look
at sun, moon, and stars? His eyes are
turned within. He sees nothing but
pools and combinations, stocks, bonds,

mortgages, bulls, bears, corners, shorts,
margins. His face is wire-drawn, anxious, does not respond to yours unless
he sees business in your eye. Fortu-
nate, if he can go home to his slippers
and paper, or his prayer-meeting, and
not dream all night of what has filled
his thoughts all day. So far as the
forgetting of all Gods but Mammon
goes, this gentleman is as Epicurean as
Epicurus ; but has he the least idea of
pleasure in any sense of the word?
That is the bitterest irony of his lot,
that he accumulates and accumulates
— and what for? The little delights of
life are spoiled for him by absorption
in business, the great seem mere extravagance ; and truly the last condition of that man is worse than the
first.

Nor can there be any question about
the supply of paganism. It does not,

indeed, run riot in the streets. The
flaunting worship of the older gods and
the wild revelry of Dionysus have given
place to labour-manifestations and the
parades of the Salvation Army. This
incapacity for pleasure that I have just
referred to hinders many a pagan from
following out the desire of his heart
which frames itself instinctively in the
old burden : Eat, drink, and be merry,
for to-morrow we die. Yet the spirit
of the decaying pagan world is everywhere. We cling with voluptuous terror
to the delights of this life, not knowing
what may come after in the dark gulf
which science points out before us. And
this paganism is found, perhaps, less in
the middle class, where inherited conventions have a stronger hold ; less in
New England, where life is built on a
more artificial model. It is the vast
lower stratum, which in this country is

always pressing upward, the half-educated multitude suddenly let loose from the bonds and trammels of an older civilization, conscious of new life, of new strength, and at the same time touched by no religion, by no care or thought for morals or for love — it is this vast, disorderly mob which is essentially pagan, and which never having tasted the pleasures of this world, knows not their vanity, and labours passionately to possess itself of them. This is not the paganism of the rich and idle, but the terrible, hungry paganism of the poor, raging like fierce beasts of prey. Communism is paganism, anarchism is paganism, latent paganism, threatening to dissolve society in a mist of blood and tears.

But we do not forget that our Epicurean is neither materialist nor pagan. He loves money as the means of procuring almost everything in this world. He loves pleasure in every form and pursues it with the keenest zest, but a large part of his pleasure consists in contemplation, and his training has generally been such that everything brutal is revolting to him. It is just here that we come across the peculiarity of the American type. For what distinguishes American Epicureanism, as well as many other American varieties, is the combination of vast scepticism with a strong habit of inherited morality, not to say religion. Are we not, indeed, as a nation a rather curious spectacle of strong moral principles which go back for their origin two or three hundred years, crusted about a body of theoretical or practical agnosticism with which they have nothing to do? Are not our churches apologetic, our creeds hidden with a cloud of ex-

planation? Are not our priests largely
occupied with the attempt to show
that our fathers did not believe what
every one knows they did believe, though
we do not? At any rate, the American
Epicurean believes very little indeed,
though he has no desire to parade his
unbelief, partly because it would result
in his own discomfort, and partly because he may come to believe a good
many things some day. At the same
time he has a habit of morals which
restrains him usually from any gross
fault, — indiscretion, he would call it.
He looks upon a thief very much as
he looks upon a dog who steals a bone
from another dog, yet he feels the most
uncomfortable qualms of conscience
if he forgets to return a borrowed
umbrella. His theories of pleasure and
of virtue are those of a joyous and
Falstaffian debauchee; but his air and

manner are sometimes hard to distinguish from those of a professor or
even of a saint. He looks with a mild
and contemptuous indifference on all
forms of government and political ques-
tions ; yet he is oftentimes a useful and
occasionally an active citizen, in the
spirit of a French writer's excellent
paradox, *Il n'y a que le sceptique pour
être honnête homme et bon citoyen.* In
short, it is because he is made up of so
many contrasts that he is so interesting.

But, you ask, where does the Epicureanism come in? It is easy to understand the scepticism of the man you are
describing, but where are his pleasures?
Has he really more of them than the
man of business? Is not he, too, anxious, care-worn, incapacitated for entering into the sweet of life? Doubtless,
to a certain extent, he is. His enjoyment is very largely a matter of theory

instead of practice.   Nor is it wholly
on moral grounds that he flees far away
from the disorders and tempestuous passions of a worldly life.   He remembers,
alas, he is too often reminded of that
sentence of Anatole France, which may
serve as a motto for so many Epicureans of to-day : "*Je n'ai qu'un seul
plaisir et je conviens qu'il n'est pas
vif, c'est la meditation: avec un mau-
vais estomac il n'en faut pas chercher
d'autres.*"   Yes, the American Epicurean must, and does for the most part,
content himself with the pleasures of
meditation: and perhaps they are, after
all, not so much inferior to others ;
they are certainly more enduring.
There is the delight of beauty, even
if one cannot create it for oneself, the
plastic arts, music, poetry.   There is
the witchery of nature, always at hand,
always varied.   Above all, there is the

vast and shifting scene of human life.
As it was expressed for us three hundred years ago : " A mere spectator of
other men's fortunes and adventures,
and how they act their parts, which, me-
thinks, are diversely presented unto me
as from a common theatre or scene.   I
hear new news every day, and those
ordinary rumors of war, plagues, fires,
inundations, thefts, murders, massacres,
meteors, comets, spectrums, prodigies,
apparitions, of towns taken, cities be-
sieged in France, Germany, Turkey, Per-
sia, Poland, etc., daily musters and prep-
arations and such like, which these tempestuous times afford ; battles fought,
so many men slain, monomachies, ship-
wrecks, piracies, and sea-fights, peace,
leagues, stratagems, and fresh alarms.
. . . New books every day, pamphlets,
currantoes, stories, whole catalogues of
volumes of all sorts, new paradoxes,

opinions, schisms, heresies, contro-
versies in philosophy, religion, etc.
Now come tidings of weddings, mask-
ings, mummeries, entertainments, jubi-
lees, embassies, tilts and tournaments,
trophies, triumphs, revels, sports, plays ;
then again, as in a new shifted scene,
treasons, cheating tricks, robberies,
enormous villainies in all kinds, funer-
als, burials, deaths of princes, new discoveries, expeditions ; now comical,
now tragical matters. To-day we hear
of new lords and officers created, to-
morrow of some great men deposed,
and then again of fresh honours con-
ferred ; one is let loose, another im-
prisoned ; one purchaseth, another
breaketh ; he thrives, his neighbour
turns bankrupt ; now plenty, then
again dearth and famine ; one runs,
another rides, wrangles, laughs, weeps,
etc. Thus I daily hear and such like,

both private and public news. Amidst
the gallantry and misery of the world :
jollity, pride, perplexities and cares,
simplicity and villainy ; subtlety, knav-
ery, candour, and integrity, mutually
mixed and offering themselves, I rub
on, *privus privatus.*" These are the
words of an intellectual Epicurean of a
former age. But I am going to repeat
to you what was said to me in confidence the other day by a friend, who is
an American Epicurean, and who, being
somewhat older than I, conceives that
he is privileged to lay down the law for
my benefit.

" My dear Sir," he said, " I have no
desire to preach to you, for I am too
inconsistent and wandering to have a
pretentious philosophy; but if you like
to profit by my experience, you may.
When I was your age, indeed, from the
time I began to think much about any-

thing, I had vast literary enthusiasms, immense ambition; I adored beauty with the idolatry of Keats, I consecrated myself to the service of letters with the passion of Flaubert, I was going to write immortal works, poems, novels, criticism; I lived, in short, in a sort of delirium. As a result of this, all the ordinary pleasures of life became a burden. The society of my friends, the little distractions, the delightful nothings, which pass away idle hours, were only stumbling-blocks in the path of my aspiration. I had so much to read, so much to write, more than I could ever possibly accomplish; and all that tended to interfere with my work, was an annoyance, however charming in itself. Well, one day it came over me, 'How foolish all this is; will any reputation or success ever satisfy me? shall I not be always as

far from the goal as now ; indeed, am I
not getting farther and farther from it,
since every book I read and every page
I write, opens the possibilities of reading and study infinitely wider than they
were before ? And this might not be so
bad if I had hopes of an endless future, of possibilities of accomplishing
and perfecting in another world what I
must leave imperfect here. But with
no such hope I am wasting the sweet
of life for nothing, toiling and labouring
to a barren and unprofitable end.' You
will easily understand that I did not
begin to cry out in this fashion until
I found that the grapes hung too high
for me, that I had not the health, or
the courage, or the genius to succeed.

"Then I made up my mind that I had
had enough of it, that I would tamper
no further with vain hopes and futile
ambitions, that I would no longer live

in a prison-house of dull abstraction,
with nerves exasperated and brain out-
worn, simply to pursue an unattainable
and vanishing ideal.   I would live on
the good, solid, dusty earth and ask no
more.   And here comes in the value
of my experience for you, young friend.
For no sooner had I taken this resolu-
tion, no sooner had I abandoned hungry labour, fierce aspiration, the vain
struggle of impossible desires, when
the aspect of the world was changed,
as if by enchantment.   I who had
railed before at the monotony and bitterness of life, who had proclaimed my
pessimism from the housetops, declar-
ing that the world was stale and old,
that no pretence of diversion could
relieve the tedium of the gray hours
rolling heavily nhe after another, I,
the prophet of *ennui*, suddenly discovered that the common existence of

G

every day was but a succession of little
delights, coming often so thickly that
one is embarrassed to choose among
them. Those of my pursuits and oc-
cupations which had before seemed
to me a trivial and frivolous waste of
time, now became an endless source
of amusement and pleasure. For-
merly, when a friend dropped in for
an hour's chat, I was haunted by the
page I might have written, I fretted
and fumed over his leisurely departure. Now I take a cigar with him
and a glass of wine, put my feet on
the table, and babble about the latest
novel and the taxes. I love books —
as did Montaigne — on the shelves,
and with the delightful feeling that I
can read them when I wish to, rarely
reading them. I used to think cards
a squandering of human life, and bil-
liards a device of the devil — whom,

you remember, I did not believe in.
Now I take a cue or a hand at whist
whenever I can find any one so idle
as myself. You, my friend, who know
nothing about these things and walk
through life simply blind, as I did,
cannot realize what a wealth of joy —
in small change — you are throwing
away. You cannot stop to look at a
sunset, because you must write a son-
net on it. I thrust my hands in my
pockets and gaze till the last glow has
fled away — and then turn to amuse
myself with something else. Like the
old mystic,

" 'On some gilded cloud or flower
My lingering soul would dwell an hour.'

The laughter of children, what old Burton found so amusing, the quarrelling
of bargemen, the nodding of a blossom
in the wind, the change of shadow and

sunlight, the singing of a bird, the falling of a star, the love of young men
and the folly of old ones, the smiles
and tears of women, fashions, freaks,
politics, philanthropy, temperance and
intemperance, the vanity of men's serious pursuits, and the woful seriousness
of their vain ones, — in all these things
there is infinite matter for more than
a May morning, if only one is not
tortured and broken by preoccupations and cares that seal one's eyes
with lead.

"And the beauty of these lighter,
slighter pleasures is, that they are not
subject to disappointment. In this
endless round of small delights one
does not look forward to long, one
does not look backward to compare.
If one amusement fails, there are a
thousand others at hand ready to make
one forget it. In short, it is the old

parable of the children and the King-
dom of Heaven. Take life as a child
takes its playthings. Enjoy each one,
and be ready to pass at a moment's
notice to another. And, above all
things, do not trouble about death.
That is another advantage of this dis-
enchantment which brings a double
enchantment with it. If you are
struggling for a high ideal, if you
have a great work to accomplish, you
are in constant fear of death, of los-
ing your object, of being cut off just
as you are about to attain. There is
but one thing that can hamper or
annoy you more in your efforts than
life, and that is death. Now, this
sweet Epicureanism that I am preach-
ing to you, makes death all but an
indifferent matter. This endless round
of little interests and pleasures serves
very well to pass away the time, but

you are willing enough to leave it.
That strange curiosity with which
death tickles us has full play, so that
even in the very midst of pleasures we
are as ready as mortality can be, to lift
the black curtain and step out into dim
night. Yes, my friend, take my word
for it, the Epicureanism I recommend
to you is the Epicureanism of Epicurus
and the true philosophy of life."

I listened respectfully, and said to
myself : "It may be, I suppose, an
excellent philosophy for him who has
no better."

THE AMERICAN PHILAN-
THROPIST.

" EVERY century," says Sainte-
 Beuve, "has its hobby : that
of the nineteenth century is charity."
This does not mean that the various
moods and theories included under
that name were unknown before, but
that the nineteenth century has made
the most of them, has become absorbed
in them to a degree earlier periods
would have found it difficult to understand. Now anything peculiar to the
nineteenth century is likely to find its
fullest development in the United
States. We are people of our time,
stamped with its very form and pressure ; and we are not clogged and

retarded, as Europe is, by old habits and inherited traditions.

It is a laudable custom to attribute everything good that has appeared in the world in the last eighteen hundred years to the influence of Christianity — philanthropy included. Even those who are not quite satisfied with this method are at least obliged to admit that every great spiritual movement since the advent of Christianity is intimately connected with it. The most attractive way of representing the matter philosophically is to regard Christianity as a vital element in the great progress of the human race, at once conditioning and conditioned by the other elements that play about it. Some people, however, deny the fact of progress altogether. "We gain," they say, "in one direction; we lose in another; and humanity in its essential traits remains the same." This view requires some distinctions. It is, indeed, true that the basis of our nature, the assertion of self, which has been summed up in the reproductive instinct and the instinct of self-preservation, continues unchanged. As long as we are animals, it is difficult to conceive of anything else. But who can compare the world of to-day with the world of the Jews or the world of the Greeks and Romans and not say that the intellectual progress has been enormous? Any theory of evolution necessarily implies such a progress; but mere empirical observation surely proves it without regard to theory. Now the moral nature of man involves a combination of intellect with the animal instincts; therefore, as regards morals, if there has not been progress, there must at least have been change.

Of course, it would be absurd to deny that the elements of charity or philanthropy existed in the world before the nineteenth century, or, indeed, as far back as we know anything of history. How can we imagine a thinking human being destitute of the impulse to give bread to the hungry and to relieve the wretched from oppression? The oldest literature abounds in instances of such sympathy and tenderness. There is not, however, much evidence that the doctrine of human brotherhood, of the solidarity of mankind as such, was popular, or even known, among the Greeks, for instance. With the Romans it is something the same; but the vast extent of the Roman Empire, the multitude of different races living in harmony together under that one sway, the toleration induced by this, did much to overcome the narrowness of ancient ideas of nationality, to emphasize the value of the individual human soul. Perhaps no classical quotation is more famous than the *Homo sum: humani nil a me alienum puto.* The philosophers of the Stoic School — Seneca, Epictetus, Marcus Aurelius — exerted a great influence in the same direction; but philosophers unfortunately do not think much of those who are not philosophers — good creatures, but so ignorant! Besides, how was it possible for the brotherhood of man to make headway in a nation whose whole political system was based on slavery?

Here comes in the influence of Christianity. The most superficial examination of even traditional Christianity must show that its fundamental principle is the value of the human soul as such. " To the poor the gospel is preached." "The last shall be first, and the first last." "For I am come not to call the righteous but sinners to repentance." Here is no distinction of class, no promise held out to the great and noble only, no salvation offered as a premium to wealth or to superior intelligence. "Blessed are they that mourn, for they shall be comforted." At last there shone upon the earth a light that was to lighten spirits in darkness, and to heal those who seemed beyond all cure.

Well, Christianity, in spite of its philanthropy and its democracy, got along very comfortably with the despotism of Rome and the despotism of Constantinople, with the tyranny of the Dark Ages, and the bigotry of mediæval Catholicism. It may be said that the teachings of Christ were abused

THE AMERICAN PHILANTHROPIST. 93

rather than used by all these powers
of evil ; yet it seems strange enough
that such a tremendous influence
should not have produced a result
earlier, if its tendency was really in
the direction suggested above. The
explanation is simple enough. Christianity did, indeed, teach the absolute
equality of all men, the perfect equiva-
lence of one soul with another, whether
rich or poor, wise or unwise, but —
and here is the point — this equality
was not in relation to this world ; it
was in relation to another. It was the
application of this principle that at
once enabled the lower classes to bear
at all the terrible anarchy of the Dark
Ages and disposed them to bear it
patiently. For the peasant, who at
one blow saw house and family torn
away from him, there was at least the
consolation of feeling that all these

woes would be soon drowned in the light of a joy which was open to high and low alike, and which would come not to the oppressor, but to the oppressed. On this account Christianity may be regarded rather as — at least negatively — the enemy of political freedom and republicanism, of the attempt to improve the condition of humanity here on earth, than as the friend of all these things. For these things require a preoccupation with the affairs of this world which is apt to interfere very considerably with devotion to another. Whether justifiably or not, the formula, "Render unto Cæsar the things which are Cæsar's," has been made and can be made to support almost any kind of arbitrary government.

Therefore, it is in a sense correct to attribute the philanthropy of the

nineteenth century to Christianity, in
another sense it is incorrect. The
true account of the genesis of that
mighty force is, I think, something
like this. After the feudal oppression
of the Dark Ages we come to the
Renaissance, the awakening of the
human spirit from its lethargy of a
thousand years. The merely animal
life in this world, — brutal in its enjoyment, stupid in its misery, — the
earth-forgetting, transfiguring life in
the next world, began to give way to
a great reaction, which substituted for
the play of muscular force the application of intellect to all the varied interests of human existence as we find
it on the green earth here about us.
The old Greek and Roman civilization reappeared, modified, deepened,
and enlarged by the influence of
Christianity. Freed from the bonds

of ecclesiastical slavery and political
anarchy, men gave themselves up in
ecstasy to taking possession of all the
new sources of joy offered them by the
present and the past. A great drama
in England, Spain, and France, a great
school of painting in Italy, gave vent to
the re-awakened creative imagination
which had fed upon Greek thought,
upon Christian feeling, above all, upon
Nature and human life, as they were
presented to human life then and
there. This gorgeous carnival lasted
longer in some countries than in others, but it lasted everywhere in its general effects through the sixteenth and
seventeenth centuries down to the
eighteenth. Then there was a cool-
ing off. The glow of imagination
faded a little, and reflection, coming
to look into things, found that the
world was not yet altogether perfect;

indeed, in many respects quite far from
it. It was evident that art and the charm
of society were very well for those who
could get them ; but there seemed to
be such a large portion of humanity
that never did get them, was, in fact,
quite as badly off as when these things
were not heard of in the world at all.

Here we come to the dawn of
modern philanthropy. The theoretical
doctrines on the subject came from
Rousseau and the philosophers of the
eighteenth century. Those philosophers were no friends to the Christian
Religion, and to give them all the
credit in the matter might seem like
disregarding the part of Christianity
altogether. The fact is, however, simply this : Rousseau and his friends
took from the religion of Jesus the
essential principle of the equality of all
men, but as their eyes were fixed on

H

this world rather than on the other, they applied it to the affairs of this world, as Christianity never had cared to do.

With the eighteenth century, then, the history of philanthropy begins, that is, of the doctrine of the universal brotherhood of man, of the elevation of the race as a whole, of the sacred right of all men to certain elementary privileges, of the duty and pleasure of associating others with one's own joys, of associating oneself with others' suffering and misery. It is impossible to separate this moral doctrine from the political theories that have resulted in universal suffrage; and the best guarantee of the permanence of the political theories is the impossibility of any return from the moral standpoint. How can the civilized world ever go back to the idea

that one class of men exists only for
the benefit of another? The theory
of political equality may prove very
difficult of application, so difficult that
a state of things quite opposed to this
theory may be brought about here
and there again and again. But nothing short of the complete extinction
of our present civilization can make
mankind forget the lesson it has been
so long in learning.

Other elements besides reasoning
do, however, enter into the doctrine
of human fellowship. The restless
imagination of the Renaissance set
itself at first to create innumerable
beings in the world of art, beings
that might afford an outlet for its
new tide of passionate emotion. But
after this resource was partially exhausted, or, more properly, after restlessness and curiosity had spread from

the artists among those who had no
particular creative gift, a flood of
human sympathy began to pour over
the whole of animate and inanimate
nature. The mind, grown too vast, too
noble for any satisfaction that the
body, the life of the immediate individual, could afford it, longed to ex-
tend its sphere of sensation, to feel
not only in its own limited range
but in the personality of others, nay,
in the vast and varying forms and
moods of nature. The literature of
the end of the eighteenth century and
the beginning of our own, the so-
called romantic movement, is a proof
of this. When had there ever been
before such an enthusiasm for reviv-
ing the history and the life of the
past, when had there been such a
passion for the natural world, such a
wild, strange longing for identification

with the life of life, for some escape
from the narrow, confining prison of
ourselves? The Greeks had been content with the calm and moderate enjoyments offered by social and national
existence. The men of the Renaissance had thrown themselves feverishly
but yet joyously into the whirl of the
senses. But the Sénancours, the Cha-
teaubriands, the Byrons, the Shelleys,
looked and longed for some satisfaction
not to be found here, some larger,
deeper grasp on being than is possible
with the limitations of our sensual
bodies. In the words of the profoundest of them: "The jonquil or
the jessamine would be enough to tell
us that such as we are we might
sojourn in a better world."

The restlessness, the fever, of that
generation has passed away. A philosophical acceptance of limitations has

spread more and more widely. The intellect, attempting no more to take the senses with it in its wanderings, has turned into the ways of science, has schooled itself to understand nature rather than feel it, to accept, since perforce it must, analysis instead of passion, curiosity instead of sympathy. Only the keen apprehension and comprehension of other people's lives can never be lost. We may not succeed very well in entering into their pleasures; but we are condemned, so long as the world shall endure, to feel their pain.

It is the combination of abstract doctrines as to the rights of man with this infinite sympathy, this acute sensibility, that makes philanthropy the swift and mighty force it grows to be. All of us, so many of us, at any rate, say with Shelley:

"Me who am as a nerve o'er which do creep
The else unfelt oppressions of this earth."

We realize in our very bodies the
suffering of the poor and wretched, to
an extent beyond the conception of
a Greek, or Roman, or Elizabethan.
We are ready sometimes to cry in
despair with Sénancour : " How can a
life be happy passed in the midst of
those who suffer? " Even the calmest
and sanest have at times an uneasiness,
almost a sense of guilt, when they find
themselves comfortable and well-off
with poverty and misery about them.

Nowhere, probably, is this tendency
so strong, nearly so strong, as it is in
America. In Europe, inherited distinctions of class make certain differences natural to the rich and tolerable
to the poor. Here we all feel that the
very theory of our government demands
equality, not only political but social;

and the struggle to maintain it is passionate.   Another thing that makes
philanthropy a prominent feature of
our civilization, is the new and immense activity of women.   The great
amount of practical energy brought
out in them by education, combined
with their natural sensibility and enthusiasm, makes them leaders and guides
in all humanitarian movements.   When
they do not take the control of things
into their own hands, they stand in
the background and urge on the men.
How many objects which men have
deemed hopeless have been attained
by the indomitable idealism, the tire-
less persistence, of women !

Certainly, the philosopher of three
hundred years ago would note among
us first of all the extraordinary number
of charitable societies, of private benevolent institutions of all kinds.   There

is no end to them : missionary societies
abroad among all nations and among
all classes at home, temperance societies, associated charities, societies for
the aid of men, of women, of children, soldiers, sailors, animals, societies to protect the uncontaminated and
convert the corrupt, societies to do
anything and everything that the imagination of man — or woman — can in-
vent, and his ingenuity execute. The
extension of this universal sympathy
beyond man, even to animals, is well
known, as are also the immense results
achieved in that direction. For the
logical extreme of this we must go to
the episode in the *Light of Asia*, where
Buddha is represented as offering his
life-blood to quench the thirst of an
exhausted tiger. The Occidental not
only shrinks from this ; his serene good-
sense teaches him to laugh at it. Nev-

ertheless, it shows that philanthropy, or rather self-renunciation, has its limitations, and perhaps is not such a universal panacea as, like other hobbies, it is sometimes assumed to be.

In short, no amount of sentiment will cover up the fact that the principle of absolute self-sacrifice is based on a contradiction. The first instinct of the human animal, like every other, is the satisfaction of immediate desire,—appetite, if you will. The development of the intellectual faculties, however, soon shows the insufficiency of any satisfaction appealing only to the senses. The next step is to construct an ideal of happiness beyond and outside of this present world, which shall be attained by the subdual and humiliation of desire in this, by self-sacrifice and even martyrdom. The enthusiasm of primitive Christianity, of mediæval

Christianity, was based on such a system. But a further process of development shows the insufficiency of even this postponement of happiness, and higher and more sensitive natures begin to repudiate distinctly the idea of buying a selfish bliss in the future by self-sacrifice in the present. Good must be done, not for gain, but for the sake of doing it. We are here, as I heard said the other day, to live for others, to be useful to the world as a whole ; when we cease to be so, we have no right to live at all. After traditional Christianity has been abandoned, even after all definite belief in dogmatic religion has faded away, we find people making out of this devotion to others a new religion, with the high-sounding name of Altruism. It is said that the child of a philosopher, hearing one day much lecturing on this subject of living for others, commented as follows : " But, Papa, if everybody is to live for others, who are the others?" Out of the mouths of babes and suck-ings —

It must be kept in mind that the principles of this religion are not those of Christianity, though they may accord with them in some points : the Christian renounces self that he may regain it more fully and freely, but there is an immense difference between this self-renunciation and self-annihila-tion. You become supremely indif-ferent to everything on earth, you become very misty about heaven ; but other people are less sceptical — why not give them all the happiness one can? Nineteenth century philanthropy is closely connected with a colossal indifference, also peculiar to the nine-teenth century, a world-weariness, not passionate, not despairing, not blasé, but simply indifferent, which sums up its philosophy in this direful phrase : "The ideal of life is to be able to have whatever you want and to want nothing whatever." O, poor humanity, which, seeing strewn before it the gray ashes of burnt-out pleasures, deludes itself a little longer by bustling about to fan, if possible, the lingering coals into a glow !

Of course, neither this indifferentism nor genuine ideal enthusiasm accounts for all philanthropy. Self is not so entirely dead among those who busy themselves with the welfare of others. We must allow something to the imperative demand for activity that is born in us, the constant and intense need of applying our mental energy to one form or another of the stolid resistance offered by nature animate or inanimate. In the

Middle Ages this restless force ex-
pended itself in destruction. Those
who to-day are philanthropists and save
lives in the fourteenth century destroyed
them. Would not Hotspur have made
an admirable philanthropist,—Hotspur,
" that kills me some six or seven dozen
of Scots at a breakfast, washes his
hands, and says to his wife : ' Fie upon
this quiet life ! I want work ' "? How
often one is disgusted with the egotism,
the arrogance, the pettiness of philanthropists. With what righteous scorn
they affect to regard any one who goes
his own way quietly, peacefully, not
injuring the rest of mankind and not
over-anxious to destroy himself in their
service ! And what supreme confidence has the philanthropist in his
methods, what sovereign indifference
for the methods of nature ! After one
has suffered and suffered long under

this infliction, can there be balm more delicious than Emerson's quiet sentence : " Nature will not have us fret and fume. She does not like our benevolence or our learning much better than she likes our frauds and wars. When we come out of the caucus, or bank, or the Abolition-convention, or the Temperance-meeting, or the Transcendental club into the fields and woods, she says to us, 'So hot? my little Sir?'"

The truth is, now that war is done away with, at least for the time, our civilization offers no sufficient equivalent. Trade — that more systematic but quite as pitiless struggle — is too slow, too barren of occasions for distinction, too openly and evidently egotistical. War, though founded on hatred, does breed a spirit of union for one cause, does afford numberless oppor-

tunities for heroism, for all the higher
and purer virtues of self-sacrifice.
Trade in itself fosters only one thing,
pure, cold, calculating selfishness, and
encourages a system of morality which
gains nothing whatever by comparison
with that of war. Indeed, it is curious
to notice how there has grown up side
by side with philanthropy and from the
same source a doctrine and method of
life entirely opposed to it, the most extreme and intense individualism. Men
are all equal : well, then let each one
take care of himself. Equal rights
imply equal ability to defend those
rights. Society is a mutual arrange-
ment by which every man is enabled;
the most fully to struggle with every
other man for material advantages, not
a vast organization in which each person plays his subordinate part for the
benefit and happiness of the whole.

There cannot be too much insistence on the immense distinction between republicanism — as conceived by Plato, for instance — and democracy, between the State as an ideal, organic principle, and individualism, or in its logical extreme, anarchy.

Now in many cases philanthropy, enthusiasm for benevolent objects, is but a cover for this tendency to individualism, to colossal selfishness. Men whose whole lives are spent in a passionate struggle, their hand against every man's, and every man's against them, compound with conscience by giving a thousand, or a great many thousand dollars, or even what is more, their time, to this or that missionary society or charitable institution. It is so much easier even to sell all one has and give to the poor than to overcome this lurking, poisoning, tempting, mas-

I

tering devil, self. Money is so much
easier to give than love. But here we
have our Emerson again in a passage
that has been a puzzle and bewilder-
ment to many a gentle and generous
soul :

" I tell thee, thou foolish philanthropist, that I grudge the dollar, the dime,
the cent I give to such men as do not
belong to me and to whom I do not
belong. There is a class of persons
to whom by all spiritual affinity I am
bought and sold ; for them I will go to
prison if need be ; but your miscel-
laneous popular charities ; the education at college of fools ; the building
of meeting-houses to the vain end to
which many now stand ; alms to sots,
and the thousand-fold Relief Societies ;
— though I confess with shame I sometimes succumb and give the dollar,
it is a wicked dollar, which by and

by I shall have the manhood to with-
hold."

In good truth there are times when
one grows infinitely weary of this cant,
which persists in taking the manner for
the matter, the letter for the spirit, the
hand for the heart.

Is there, then, nothing more to be
said? After such a cold analysis, is
there no palinode to be sung? It
seems almost a crime to sit idly in
one's study and dissect, perhaps falsely,
at any rate uselessly, the most real, the
most lasting, the most ennobling of all
the interests that make life beautiful or
even tolerable. It is not the great
movements that count, the noise, the
ostentatious self-sacrifices, the flaunting
self-conscious activity; it is the quiet
lives of daily renunciation and denial,
the lives that are passed in shadow,
devoted to soothing pain, to ending

strife, to spreading love by sweet example, without reward, often unconsciously. Who can overlook it, or resist it, or put it away from him? we are not men, but man. What you have suffered I may suffer, do suffer; what you enjoy, enjoy. Do we not all, all come back to those words of Shelley,

" Me who am as a nerve o'er which do creep
  The else unfelt oppressions of this earth " ?

He whose nerves do not thrill and throb and burn at the thought of tyranny or injustice — injustice of humanity or the still fiercer injustice of circumstances — is not a man, but a machine, does not exist. When we are away from home, faces indifferent there, or even disagreeable, become sweet and full of kinship. So must it be for man with man in the wide, uncertain desert of this world. As shipwrecked sailors, in their hour of calm and prosperity separated by jarring interests, by petty quarrels, are yet knit together in one great terror before the face of death ; so we, as we look at our individual, earthly existences, feel no connection, no sympathy ; but when we turn and meet the invisible, the un-known in which these frail habitations, our bodies, are swayed like a bubble in the wind, we cling together mutely, passionately, sustained by that love alone in the dim gulf of an enormous night.

THE AMERICAN MAN OF LETTERS.

IT is difficult to define the man of letters. He is one who lives for literature, and generally by literature, who makes it a serious pursuit and no pastime; not a specialist, though he sometimes deals with specialties; nor a scholar, though he is sometimes deeply read in many things. If he writes on philosophy or history, he must have a sense of style, of dramatic construction and effect. Plato was a man of letters, but can one say the same of Aristotle? Tacitus was, and Gibbon; but one hesitates to apply the name to Mommsen or to the late E. A. Freeman.

There are some poets who hardly seem to be men of letters, — singers of spontaneous and flowing genius, who write as they breathe, and have apparently no consciousness of effort: Shakspere, Chaucer, Byron, Scott even, in spite of his enormous production and the labour involved in it. Virgil, on the other hand, Dante, Milton, above all, Goethe, are men of letters first, poets afterward.

I have named a classical and a mediæval writer. Such men as Lucian or Erasmus have certainly much of the modern man of letters about them. Yet it is with the seventeenth century only that the type fully develops its qualities. Dryden is an admirable example: ready to turn his hand to anything, swift in production, easy in manner, free from pedantry, yet accurate, and careful of pure diction;

proud of his profession, not treating it as a plaything, like Byron and Scott, yet a man of the world, with his eyes open to what went on about him. And in France we have Voltaire, to whom pedantry was of all things most abhorrent, yet who never let his pen dangle nor forgot his art. The ideal man of letters stands halfway between the poet and the literary hack: he envies the poet's divine fire, but dreads his frenzy; he scorns vulgarity and the hasty patching of the penny-a-liner.

The journalist is not necessarily a man of letters, but the growth of journalism has made a great difference in the literary career. Before the days of periodical literature men wrote for a small, cultivated class, whose criticism was always more or less intelligent; they had not the

pressure of a yawning column waiting to be filled   This hurry of publication suits some quick and active
minds, which work readily, perhaps
work best, under the spur; but it is
not favourable to long, silent, patient
labour on a masterpiece.   It is so
easy now for the best writers to slip
into criticism, into facile, graceful
comment on the works of others!
The magazines are open, and pay
well; easy writing makes easy reading; the public prefer what they can
catch at an idle moment, in a car,
between two naps.   Perhaps great
geniuses do not fall into this error,
but it is strange if they do not.   At
any rate, we are flooded with books
well worth reading, full of talent,
which may not be slighted, yet ephemeral, not only from haste of compo-
sition, but from their exclusive appeal

to the taste of the day. Take, in French literature, for instance, Sainte-Beuve, a man of the most original genius, penetrating insight, grace and poetry of style. He has been dead twenty odd years, and how old-fashioned he seems beside the French criticism of to-day! I do not mean that MM. Brunetière, Faguet, Lemaître, France, are his superiors in knowledge or skill, but they are near to us, and he is remote, — as they will be twenty-five years hence.

The modern man of letters — especially if we confine ourselves to the poet, novelist, dramatist, or critic — is sorely tried by the need of deciding between two alternatives. On the one hand he has before him the literature of the past, a huge, silent treasure-house, which he must explore more or less, which he can never ran-

sack thoroughly, which, if he has the
conscience of his art, perpetually
haunts him. On the other hand he
has the spectacle of life, — life infinitely varied, as in the modern world
it is, in any world, — the bewilder-
ing beauty of colour and movement,
the endless play of human passions on
each other, the million new shapes in
which old traits appear, morals and
immorals, the one as interesting as
the other, and none of these things to
be neglected. He needs the books
to throw light on the world, he must
have the world to vivify the books.
How can he have both? The modern
literature of Germany amply shows the
lack of the one. And those very
French critics I have been speaking
of show the want of the other; for,
varied and charming as they are, one
does not find them very deep in in-

tellectual matters. Even when they are familiar with their own literature, it is really astonishing to an American to see how ignorant they are of the literatures of other countries. Yet in the nineteenth century, to know one literature one must know all.

The tendencies of modern literary life in France are illustrated in an interesting way in the Journal of the brothers De Goncourt, whose intimate and long-continued collaboration is one of the most curious cases of a curious phenomenon. They were men who chose their course early. The past had little interest for them and was soon cast aside. Except in one or two periods history had no lessons for them. They cared only to keep their eyes and ears open to what went on about them, to rivet all their senses on the subtle yet significant phases of contemporary life. By this method they succeeded in obtaining very curious, in some respects very admirable, results; but their narrowness and lack of sympathy annoys one constantly.

Another difficulty for the man of letters: there has never before been any such competition as he is obliged to contend with to-day. It is easy to say that good work will always come to the front, that genius will make its way. But there are different kinds of good work. The public has never been so composite as it is now. Before the universal triumph of democracy literature was controlled by educated people. They may not have done all the reading, but they did all the deciding. If they pronounced anything good, the herd took that or nothing at all. Now every one is educated so that there are no longer educated people. What is of more importance, every one is busy. Literary work, to reach permanence, must fight its way through the mob of weary men and women who read to be amused in the easiest and most superficial manner. It must not only have abiding qualities of originality and power; it must have superficial attractions, which are not always combined with such qualities.

In other words, the candidate for literary honours has to compete not only with genius but with mediocrity. This must have been always the case to a certain extent, but it is of the greatest consequence to-day. The career of a novelist like M. Georges Ohnet in France illustrates what I mean. He is apparently an author of great cleverness, with an easy grace of manner, and a faculty of writing to please the average man because he resembles him. Well, his success has been enormous. He sells not only editions, but tens of editions with perfect ease, and it is amusing to watch the wrath and scorn of the French critics to whom it falls to judge him. Possibly names of the same kind might be picked out for England and America.

One great advantage that mediocrity has in this race is fertility of production. This is not always denied to genius, as we see in the cases of Scott and George Sand, though it is to be wished that even they had yielded a little less to the pressure of popularity. But evidently fertility is not a necessary element of great literary power, and to write hurriedly is certainly not the best way to write well. Now, writers like M. Georges Ohnet, and many others, whom I need not name, can produce their literary wares, such as they are, as readily as they breathe. The limit to their work is set only by their industry and their physical strength. Conscientious, thoughtful, painstaking writers can not for a moment compete with them.

Imagine a young man who begins with a determination to make literature a profession, the business of his life. He has high ideals, original views of things. He has prepared himself by careful study of great thinkers and great masters of style, and he is ready to study much more, to make his work solid and worthy of a place among the books he worships.

He says to himself: "I will not trifle
with what is ephemeral. I will not
condescend to cheap work, hack work,
hasty work. I will not degrade my
genius, if I have one, by that of which
I should hereafter be ashamed."
What is such a man to do? If he is
poor and must earn his living, his
position is worst of all. But even
suppose him so situated that this is
not absolutely necessary. He must
get his name before the public and
keep it there. Thoughtful, serious
criticism will not do this for him.
Even fiction will not do it, unless he
has some special rattle for the public
imbecility. Poetry, if it were com-
posed by all the nine Muses together,
would never reach the light of day.
I remember seeing it stated not long
ago, and I have no doubt correctly,
that there is not a publisher in Amer-

K

ica who will take any risk with poetry by an unknown author. Perhaps this has been always more or less true. Certain kinds of literature have never had an extensive sale when first produced; but supposing the sale of them to have been in times past no larger than it is to-day, — and very likely it was not so large, — the damning fact is that they are choked at once by the enormous mass of more popular work put in competition with them. It may be that the wheat has never prospered more abundantly than now, but the crop of tares has increased a million fold.

Our young author, therefore, yields to the temptation to sow tares of his own, thinking that, just as people plant quick-springing grain to protect their lawns, and then get rid of it afterwards, so he can bring forward

his good matter under cover of his
trash, and with years transform himself from a jack-of-all-trades to a
passed master in the highest province
of art.   It may happen so sometimes.
More frequently the man who thus
sets out falls more and more under
the rod of public tyranny.   If he succeeds in a popular line, it is hard to
give it up.   If he fails, he is tied to
the wheel indefinitely.   In any case,
he awakes some day to find his style
disfigured and corrupted, his ideas
scattered and deformed, his confidence in human nature wofully
shaken, his great literary ideal faded
and vanished, he knows not where.

But suppose he avoids this danger,
and, instead of putting on the yoke,
chooses an eremitic or Bohemian
wretchedness, with only his ideal to
adore.   Suppose he avoids the mam-

mon of popularity and closets himself with some great work, which,
once published, shall bring him fame
and riches and everything that is
desirable.   In the first place, a great
work carried on under these conditions is apt to come to nothing.
Without the spur of definite hope, a
man in such a case procrastinates
until the ideal of success seems so
far off that he prefers to nurse it for
itself rather than risk the loss of it
altogether.   Even if he perseveres,
overcomes poverty and sickness and
heart-sickness by indomitable will,
makes his work his pleasure and shuns
everything that does not tend to forward it and perfect it, — well, are the
chances great that he will ever get it
before the world, or that, when he has
dragged it from publisher to publisher, and at last found a reluctant

acceptance, he will ever get more for
it than scanty praise and scantier
pence? Of course, this "mute, in-
glorious Milton" sort of thing is generally rejected; people say that really
inspired production is always recognized. Perhaps it is; but how do
they know it?

The truth is, the uncertain fortunes
of literary work are a melancholy fact.
Not to mention the shifting fame of
even Dante or Shakspere, take Shelley, who paid for the publication of
his own poems, take these same De
Goncourts I mentioned above, who
also paid for the publication of their
earlier novels, and who afterwards
stood among the first writers of the
school. Perhaps one ought not to say
that everything refused by publishers
is good, but one may safely infer that
much is so. Not that they can be

blamed. Plenty of people to-day speak with enthusiasm of *David Grieve;* yet there are also plenty of critics who, if one judges by their tone, would not accept it offered them by an unknown writer.

There are chances in all these things. Flaubert worked years over *Madame Bovary,* putting into it almost incredible labour and care. It had an enormous success. Nevertheless, in the De Goncourts' Journal we find him complaining bitterly that what made *Madame Bovary* succeed was its *côté vaudeville,* that is its having what the French commonly call a success of scandal. Indeed, no one could for a moment imagine that either *La Tentation de Saint Antoine, Salammbô,* or *L'Éducation Sentimentale* would have made any impression on the public, if *Madame Bovary* had not preceded them.

Those who do not mind the harsh
and monotonous pessimism of Leopardi will find in his essay called
Il Parini ovvero Della Gloria a vigorous and passionate statement of the
difficulties with which the modern
man of letters has to contend. Leopardi himself failed in the struggle
with them, or at least he could not
overcome them during his lifetime;
and what he thought of posthumous
reputation the reader will learn from
the essay referred to above.

What I have said thus far is general, and does not especially bear on
American conditions. One or two
things make the position of the American man of letters quite different
from that of his French or English
brother. In the first place, — though
it takes courage to say so, — our public is more ignorant. That is easily

explained.   The public here includes a far greater part of the population than in European countries.   Such magazines as *Harper's* and *The Century* are read by every one.   They must therefore contain matter that every one can read.   I have heard that the editor of a magazine more literary in character than either *Harper's* or *The Century* aims to take nothing which will not be alike intelligible to his butcher and to a college professor.   The taste of one may be as good as that of the other, but it is something of a strain to have to address oneself to both.   The late James Russell Lowell is credited with saying that we were "the most common-schooled and the least educated people in the world."   I doubt whether that is true.   But it is probable that education, taken in the sense not of common-schooling nor of mere scholarship, but of thoughtful, trained knowledge of human life based on a familiar acquaintance with both the past and the present, never had less influence over the fortunes of literature, at any rate, and perhaps of some other things, than it has in the United States to-day. With this condition of affairs the American man of letters has to contend. Well is it for him, if he succeeds, as Lowell in a measure did, in combining a talent for catching the ear of the great, indolent, capricious public with solid learning, original thought, and literary charm. Without the first of these requisites he will give up his pursuit in disgust, or he will struggle vainly, wearily, and wreck at last, unhonoured and unknown.

Another difficulty the American

man of letters has to overcome. He
has no literature behind him. It is
hardly possible for one who has not
given himself to a literary life to imagine what this means. The French
or English historian, critic, novelist,
poet, has an immense past from which
he can draw matter sure to be interesting to his public, sure to command
a certain amount of sympathy from
its very nature. A critic like Sainte-
Beuve — and, indeed, like most of
those of contemporary France — may
bury himself entirely in French literature, may know little or nothing of
the literature of other countries, and
have by that very fact a better claim
on the attention of his public. The
same is true of models as of matter.
A Frenchman or Englishman has
behind him the great masters of his
own literature, the study of whom is

connected with all the circumstances of his own intellectual development. Every reminiscence of them is sure to be familiar and acceptable to his readers. Every association with them gives an added charm to any work of his own.

It will be said that we have at any rate two hundred years of history behind us. It is very true, and of late excellent use has been made of it. But if we take out two or three wars, some of those not the most exciting ever heard of, no one will, I think, maintain that our past is picturesque when compared with that of Europe in the last two centuries; nor has there been till very recently the variety of manners or the movement of life which is absolutely essential to literary work intended to interest the general public.

For models, however, we are much
worse off than for historical material.
Irving and Cooper, Prescott and Mot-
ley, are excellent writers, no doubt;
but there are not many more like
them, and no one will, I think, place
them with Shakspere or Voltaire.
We usually think of the literature of
England as belonging to us also; but
any one who has tried it knows how
hard it is to keep up this fiction, how
jealous people are inclined to be of
what is English, how far away from us
English manners and interests are,
while they are growing more distant
every day.

There ought to be some advantages
in not being hampered by a tradition
inherited from the past. If we have
no models to work from, we should in
all fairness have no standards to be
judged by. This is not, I think,

practically the case. A great part of
our literature consists of imitations
of old-world celebrities. And the
new schools which struggle after originality are apt to show a painful effort
in the pursuit of it. Whitman, for
instance, is a man of genuine power;
yet it is hard to tell whether he is
more affected in his departure from
recognized standards or in his unconscious reproduction of them.

It will be asked why any one goes
into literature at all, when the pros-
pect is so unattractive. But the
answers — there are a number of them
— are ready. In the first place, the
literary life is supposed by the out-
sider to be an easy life. It is not an
easy life, but people are tempted into
it on that supposition. It is a com-
paratively free life. That is, you
must work all the time, but you need

work only when you wish to, if the paradox be permissible. At any rate, you have no one in authority over you.

It is a life that requires no training, or at least on this point also many are misled by the popular idea of it. It is certainly a lottery in which the prizes are very great, and in which they may and do fall where they are least expected, if not least deserved. In the other arts one never succeeds without prolonged and patient effort. In literature cases have been known where great success attended the first attempt. Most of us have a good opinion of our own powers before we have tried them. Why should not we startle the world as well as others?

Great is the love of reputation. It is agreeable to be bowed down to, and in this country especially, a small amount of literary distinction goes a great way. The popular corres- pondent of a newspaper, who very possibly cannot spell, gets much more incense than the author of a treatise on philosophy. And where reputa- tion, numerical glory, is the object, — with whom is it not an object of greater or less account? — what more dazzling ideal could be proposed than literary success in the United States. A public quantitatively so great was never addressed by an author before. A novelist, a novelist who attains notoriety, can, I sup- pose, count on millions of readers. Compared with the successes of two hundred years ago, it really seems like writing for posterity in your own day.

Naturally, then, a good many men, and a good many women, go into lit-

erature, and as they go into it with
their eyes open, perhaps they deserve
no pity when they fail. Still, some
of them cherish the amiable delusion
that they are giving their lives to
benefit the human race, and one cannot refuse them a certain amount of
sympathy. Indeed, in so far as they
keep this ideal before them, they are
surely worthy of all respect and admi-
ration. The man who refuses to sacrifice his literary conscience, who
refuses to bow down before the altar
of cheap sensationalism, trivial gos-
sip, machine politics, who does these
things not only from perhaps fantastic
notions about the service of art for
art, but from a sense of personal
dignity and self-respect, that man,
whether successful or unsuccessful,
deserves all honour, more than in
many instances he gets. He is the

ideal American man of letters, and I might have dwelt more fully on him. His office is, or should be, a most important one, and he must strive with all the power in him to make it so.

One writer we have had who took this position in an almost ideal way; I mean Emerson. Emerson was not, indeed, a man of letters in the narrowest sense. He was more than that. He was a prophet, a sage, an inspirer of other men, who used literature, sometimes a little impatiently, as an imperfect instrument for imparting the truths he felt himself destined to convey. But he had many qualities the man of letters would do well to imitate. He was essentially a modern man. He was familiar with the past and loved many things about it; but he was "up to the times" in the fullest sense, in science, in theology,

L

in politics. He looked forward and not back; it cannot be too often emphasized. Besides this, he was a lover of truth and had his eyes open to seek it. In this he recalls another great writer, who from some points of view may serve as the model man of letters, Goethe. He it was who wrote that sentence which should be the motto — one of the mottoes — of every one who devotes himself to a literary life: " *Wahrheitsliebe zeigt sich darin, dass man überall das Gute zu finden und zu schätzen weiss.*" Love of truth, hatred of insincerity and sham, whether it means courting vulgar tastes or shouting party watchwords, openness, sympathy, — these are, above all, what the man of letters should cultivate in this or in any other country. But here, where, in the uncertain state of creeds and churches, he becomes a sort of guide, priest almost, he should seek these things with all his heart and soul, at the same time with a clear, though somewhat melancholy, consciousness that other things will not be added unto him.

I often ask myself — probably many others do likewise — what will be the first really great original literary development of this country. I suppose no one will claim that we have, as yet, done anything worthy of our name and position in history. We have had many good authors here and there, but none of the first calibre or scope. Will the coming writer be a novelist? Certain things seem to indicate that the novel, at least in the ordinary form, has for the present had its day. Genius can do anything, but it is difficult for common minds to see how any new departure in the way of a novel is possible. And it is safe to predict — now — that the coming writer will not be in the closest sense a realist, — if anybody can say what that sense is.

Will there be a grand revival of the drama? It is difficult to imagine. In spite of some signs of improvement on the American stage, the conditions are unpromising. The supremacy of the "common-schooled" is felt far more in the theatre than in the publishing house. More than that, the theatre would seem to demand a metropolis for its successful development. It is essentially dependent upon a local atmosphere. Plays intended for a dozen capitals cannot take hold like those written for Paris. It is also argued that stage-settings are killing the drama. About that there may be more question. But it cannot be denied that there exists a separation between actors and managers on the one hand and the literary class on the other, which makes a truly literary drama seem almost hopeless.

Well — and poetry? Some people think poetry has disappeared from the world forever. I am not of that number. The enjoyment of metrical form, and the peculiar excitement of style that goes with it, do seem at a low ebb among our practical countrymen. But it has been so before. It was so in the dark ages, when the world was barbarous; it was so in the later Roman age, when the world was barbarous from over-civilization, — as it is now. But there comes a Renaissance for all these things. The Muses are, perhaps, the only deities who do not at length abandon the children of men.

Yet it is not poetry that most often suggests itself to me as the regenerator of our literary reputation. I cannot but think that the form of art which would at once be most akin to certain feelings of our people, and would also be compatible with the demands of literary excellence, would be some great work of humour, of laughter. We are too serious, we take ourselves too seriously, our vices and our virtues too seriously, life too seriously. The defect of such a writer as Whitman is that he cannot see in how many respects he is an enormous joke. We have had humourists, it is true. I am not sure but that their writings form to-day the most original and characteristic literature we have; which is not very creditable to us, for they are extremely vulgar and extremely superficial, whereas the truly great literary

humourist is free from all vulgarity
and profoundly deep. But some day,
before many years,— he may be among
us now, — there will come a true son
of Aristophanes and Rabelais and Cer-
vantes, who will prick the bubble of
our vast self-satisfaction, without
bitterness, without harshness, with
none of the cynical satire of the
French pessimistic school. His first
principle will be laughter, but his
second will be love; and he will show
that we must take this good world as.
we find it, not complain because it is
not better, nor wear all the joy out of
ourselves trying to make it better.
He will ridicule a great many things:
politics, and patent medicines, and
temperance societies, and woman's
rights, and reform generally. He will
tread on a great many people s toes,
and turn the world upside down, and

make us see the great glories of this bustling age insignificant and jumbled together like the glass in a kaleidoscope. He will spare no one, yet every one will love him, because he will be lovable, which is, after all, the best reason for loving in the world. And I should advise him to inscribe on his title-page these charming verses, which I borrow from M. Anatole France, who has himself borrowed them from I know not where, —

"Les petites marionettes
Font, font, font
Trois petits tours
Et puis s'en vont."

THE AMERICAN OUT OF DOORS.

WE are too prone to look at modern life as cut off from the past by a great gulf: it is so much more important to us. A Greek, a mediæval Italian, seems spectral, impossible. We cannot realize that Athenians and Florentines loved and hated, bought and sold, jested, wept, talked scandal, suffered and died, quite as men do nowadays. The world is so old and yet so new. These same commonplaces I am writing have been written so many times before and seemed just as common place. Yet we forget them.

Notwithstanding, certain differences, marked differences, do separate the nineteenth century from the past. Great forces have worked to mould our civilization, some of them external and material, yet even these reacting on the internal and spiritual, as the external, to a greater or less degree, always must. To go some way back, there is printing, a force that made itself felt long ago; but the development of printing in the daily press is something absolutely modern, and who can estimate its importance? Then there is democracy, closely connected with the preceding; the belief that the numerical majority of mankind is not only entitled to equal consideration by government, but competent to control that government, almost, if not quite, directly. Again, we have the great mechanical

discoveries, which fall within the last
hundred years: steam, the breaker-
down of barriers, the annihilator of
nationality, the agent that has tripled
man's control of nature and drawn
tighter the girdle of the world; elec-
tricity, which already regards tele-
graph and telephone as trifles, and
looks forward to producing in another
century a locomotive power that will
make us cast steam into a corner,
forgotten.

There are spiritual influences, too,
subtler and harder to investigate,
which may be considered either as
cause or as effect. For instance,
there is the extraordinary development of music, which in the modern
sense can scarcely be said to be three
hundred years old: music, so different from all the other arts in its combination of sensuous appeal with

supersensual suggestion; so quick to profit by mechanics, yet so far above them; so capable of expressing all moods and all passions; so various in its methods and styles; in a word, so pre-eminently modern. Another influence, quite as modern and even more powerful, is the love of nature. Perhaps I should say, the scientific study and comprehension of nature. Neither expression by itself is sufficient.

All literature and history prove that the character of a people is largely modified by the topography of the region it inhabits; and the extremes to which a theory based on this is carried by Taine and critics of his school are well known. Most nations have been conscious of the part thus taken by their surroundings in their moral development, and have

recognized it in one way or another.
This is, however, quite different from
scientific study.   Observation, the
patient search after facts, seems to
be a late fruit of civilization, a fruit
that was very long in ripening.
Socrates, at least in Xenophon's re-
port of him, anticipated Pope in proclaiming that "the proper study of
mankind is man." Aristotle, with
his immense curiosity, discovered and
recorded many things; but the natural
history of the ancients is largely fabu-
lous and *a priori*, as in the elaborate
work of Pliny; and the mass of de-
duction and hearsay transmitted by
that industrious personage influenced
the science of the Middle Ages to an
astonishing degree.   Those who are
familiar with Elizabethan writers are
well aware of this.   The extravagant
zoölogy and botany which formed an

important element in the style of
Lyly and the Euphuists have been
frequently ridiculed. Even Shakspere is by no means free, as in his

> " Sweet are the uses of adversity,
>   Which, like the toad, ugly and venomous,
>   Wears yet a precious jewel in his head."

But patient scientific study had not
been wanting in the Renaissance,
amid all the riot of the imagination.
The great voyagers and explorers,
although they brought home new fic-
tions of their own, yet destroyed many
of the old. Copernicus had revolu-
tionized astronomy, and even among
the Elizabethans his discoveries were
beginning to have their effect on the
literary world. Bacon laid the foundation of modern scientific methods,
and the temper developed rapidly, as
we see in Browne's book on Vulgar

Errors, which admits some extraordinary conclusions, but shows a true spirit of curiosity, of critical research, and of respect, at least, for thorough experiment.

In the eighteenth century such a spirit spread everywhere, as reason began to supplant imagination, and poetry to give way to prose. The eighteenth century was, however, too busy with political and social problems to concern itself seriously with great scientific movements. Philosophy and political economy, the study of man, took precedence of the study of nature. With the nineteenth century the latter pursuit finally asserted itself. The great mechanical inventions and practical applications of science increased the facilities for theoretical investigation, and made it more attractive. The theories elabo-

rated by Darwin were, as is well
known, in the air some time before
he formulated them. He is but the
representative of his age, at least in
that direction; nor would it be possible to find a better example of the
ideal scientist than he. Patient,
spending years in the accumulation
of facts, never hastening, never fret-
ting, putting results as far as possible
out of sight that they may not tempt
him from severe and unprejudiced
investigation, working for no end of
practical utility, and for fame only
carelessly and as a secondary object,
such a man personifies the best that
nature has to teach us. We learn
from him respect for details that
seem insignificant; we learn not to
jump at conclusions; we learn once
more the lesson — alas, so often forgotten — of Newton, "picking up a

shell here and there on the beach,
while the vast ocean of truth lay open
before him." Darwin is perhaps too
favourable an example of the natural-
ist's modesty and simplicity, but
familiarity with nature appears to
breed these qualities more than some
studies peculiarly associated with
man.

What could be more important than
the change produced in our view of
the external world by the theories
which are generally connected with
Darwin's name? A French critic
writes: "Is it preposterous to say
that posterity will draw a line, a deep
line, in the history of human thought,
between the men who lived before and
those who lived after Darwin? It is
somewhat as the change that was for-
merly brought about by the discovery
of America and of Copernican cos-

M

mology." Whether this feeling be
true or false, it would be foolish to
deny the immense hold it has taken
on men's minds. We may not for-
mally accept the principle of evolution, but we are all of us inclined to
put man in a very different position
in nature from the one he occupied a
hundred years ago. He is no longer
a little god, with the rest of the universe prostrate at his feet, but takes
his place among other beings, an
essential element, — the most essential, possibly, but still only an element
in the vast play of the organic and in-
organic world. Nor is this view contrary to philosophy as distinguished
from science, though the conclusion
may be reached along a different line.
To the Hegelian, as to the Darwinian,
man has ceased to be cut off and dis-
sociated from nature; she has no

reality but in him, yet neither has he reality but in her. It is evident that to a man who has accepted these doctrines the external world assumes a new aspect: it is no longer something indifferent, or an enemy to be kept under and controlled; it is an inexhaustible store of facts, each bound up with others and bearing upon them, each pregnant with its own teaching, and perhaps with a lesson that no man can afford to overlook or neglect.

I believe this new growth of interest in nature is nowhere so widespread as among the people of the United States. The Teutonic and Keltic races seem to take to it more readily than the Latin, and even than the Greek. Greek poetry is full of allusions to natural objects, but these are almost always referred to in illus-

tration of human passions. The gift
of painting in clear lines and with
imaginative feeling, as we see it, for
instance, in Theocritus, which is
characteristic of the divine Greek
genius in everything, must not be
confused with the love of description which has become conspicuous
in modern literature. Occasional
touches of outdoor life with an exquisite charm are to be found in
Lucretius, in Catullus, in Virgil; but
here, too, everything is subordinated
to man. It has been observed that
to the Romans Switzerland was merely
desolate and repulsive, which is
enough to show that they had not
the modern sense of the picturesque.
A somewhat careful study of the
Italian poet Leopardi has convinced
me that he had nothing of the peculiar sentiment of nature-worship so

striking in his contemporaries, English, French, and German. Nor do we find it in the great poets of Spain, if a conclusion on the subject be permitted to one who has only entered the skirts of the great forest of seventeenth-century drama. The plays of Calderon are full of roses and waves and winds and nightingales. It would be hard to surpass the melancholy and Virgilian grace of his flowers, —

"Durmiendo en brazos de la noche fria;"

but one does not find in him that subtle observation combined with imaginative colour which abounds in Shakspere : —

"A mole cinq-spotted, like the crimson drops
  I' the bottom of a cowslip."

"Daffodils,
That come before the swallow dares, and take
The winds of March with beauty."

The love of the Kelts for nature, and their method of interpreting her as compared with the methods of other races, are admirably analyzed in Matthew Arnold's *Lectures on Celtic Literature*, one of his most charming books. Whether it be indeed owing to a difference of race instinct, or to the close contact with the material world induced by the necessity of combat with it, the northern nations of Europe are certainly more familiar with that world than those of the south.

Familiarity with nature takes two forms, one exoteric, the other esoteric: either nature is viewed in detail, as an object of endless interest and amusement, or she is deified with a passionate and religious adoration. The first of these forms is probably more general in the United

States than it has ever before been anywhere. No other people read as we do the current literature of the day, newspapers, magazines. But that literature is kept full of scientific speculation in every form. It is in the air all about us. We imbibe the chief fact of evolution from our infancy, and look upon monkeys with a weird interest and a superstitious eye for ancestral traits. The discussion of these matters is not confined to scholars and professors; one hears it every day among men of business, even among mechanics.

We are a nation of travellers. We are not rooted and moss-grown, like Europeans. Moving house and home is the excitement of life, and a man who dies where he was born is a curiosity. Men and women work hard all their lives, and at sixty set out to

see the world.   They go to California
or Mexico or Alaska for six weeks,
like it, and make a journey to India.
In one sense, this perpetual locomo-
tion cuts us off from nature.   It inter-
feres with the forming of associations.
It abolishes the peculiar kinship that
knits up some fact of the past with
every tree and stone, making old
houses seem like old faces well beloved.   I do not think any of our
people have the attachment which, it
is said, in some European countries
binds the peasant to the soil; nor
indeed have we a peasantry, in the
European sense, anywhere within our
borders.

Yet if our acquaintance with nature
is not intimate, it is extensive.   In
almost every company you will find
people who are familiar with the
swamps of Florida and the prairies

of Kansas, the Rocky Mountains and
the Yosemite Valley. It is important
to note that in our American journey-
ing, at any rate, we look especially at
such natural objects because nothing
else is new. From Boston to San
Francisco man is substantially the
same. Variety must be sought in
nature. Curiosity can spend itself
no longer on manners and customs.
If we look from the car windows, we
have no eyes for the eternal John
Smith; he stands for insignificance
in the foreground of the picture.
The feeling thus fostered is, indeed,
often shallow and idle. These universal sight-seers have no reverence,
not even a spirit of thoughtful and
sober inquiry. The scenery they are
whirled through becomes a panorama,
a theatrical spectacle, and their only
impulse is a longing for some higher

mountain, or broader river, or wilder
valley, to rouse dull eyes once more
into a languid enthusiasm. They
have a catalogue, a collection of objects of interest, and compare notes:
"Have you been there?" "Oh, you
ought to see that!" Yet an effect remains. Petty prejudices and provin-
cial notions are partially obliterated.
You cannot come in contact with
nature even in this superficial way
without gaining something of her
largeness and her calm. There is a
gain of sympathy, also. Perhaps we
are not naturally a sporting people,
like our English cousins. If we are
so, we have lost the taste to a great
degree, and acquired a dislike for
shooting, even for fishing. We prefer to live and let live, with beast as
well as man. A simple walk is
enough for us; the sight of birds and

animals pleases us more than the destruction of them. We love the open air for itself, and are contented with it. How many of us revel in that joyous cry of Emerson, "Give me health and a day, and I will make the pomp of emperors ridiculous"!

This sweet, fresh renewal that comes from contact with nature is felt even by people who have little imagination or sensibility, who abhor solitude, and certainly would not choose the country as an abiding-place. In summer the whole population flock to the mountains and salt water, and they are not quite the same there as at home. Mr. Bradford Torrey, in his charming *A Rambler's Lease*, says: "I hope I am not lacking in a wholesome disrespect for sentimentality and affectation; for artificial ecstasies over sunsets and landscapes, birds and flowers; the fashionable cant of nature-worship, which is enough almost to seal a true worshipper's lips under a vow of everlasting silence." Certainly there is a great deal of such cant, and the canter is only too apt to go away and forget what manner of man he was. Yet even the lightest, the most frivolous, the most hardened, get something from these things. The very existence of the fashion shows a tendency.

A large class of people do, however, take the matter more seriously. The scientific views I have referred to above give the study of nature an interest which strikes deeper than a mere desultory curiosity. There are many men and women who have picked up a smattering of botany or ornithology in childhood, and find it afterwards a never-failing occupation, opening new vistas and revealing deep secrets, always within reach and always fascinating. Careful study of this kind sometimes breeds a contempt for large effects, keeps the eyes near earth on microscopic beauty; but how close it brings one to the intricate mystery of life!

Science, too, has the great advantage of being accessible in fragments, and not requiring lifelong familiarity for the appreciation of its pleasures. It is different from literature, which demands a patient apprenticeship, and is not open to the first comer. A busy man can see a great deal out of doors to interest him at odd moments; but he is not likely to make close friends of Homer and Dante.

I have not, I think, exaggerated the importance of what external nature has done and is doing for Americans; but it may be exaggerated by confusing the two forms of familiarity with natural objects that I have noted above. One hears a good deal of talk about the religion of nature, about a worship which will put aside churches and go into the woods, about a reverence which will associate itself more deeply and truly with trees and flowers and stars than with buildings fashioned by the hand of man, about a devotion bred by quiet in the fields rather than by liturgies or outgrown creeds or dim cathedrals. We must distinguish here. At the opening of this century, in the passionate reaction against the social and religious conventions of the last, poets and men of letters were strongly moved to substitute for certain traditional theories of religion a deeper, ampler, and vaguer sentiment. Beginning with Rousseau, this tendency spread to

many men of a quite different stamp.
The poets of England, France, and
Germany poured forth upon natural
objects all the ecstasies of lovers.
The beauty of colour, sound, motion,
filled them, mastered them. They
lost themselves in the sway of great
winds, in the slow majesty of midday
clouds, in the undulation of grass
floating in the summer light. English poetry will show us this better
than any other. Let us take Cowper,
still timid, still Christian in the sense
that made Sainte-Beuve say, "The
great Pan has naught to do with the
great Crucified One," yet striking
again and again notes passionate as
this : —

"Lanes, in which the primrose ere her time
Peeps through the moss that clothes the haw-
        thorn root,
Deceive no student;"

or Keats crying to the Nightingale: —

"Now more than ever seems it rich to die,
  To cease upon the midnight with no pain,
  While thou art pouring forth thy soul abroad
      In such an ecstasy;"

or Wordsworth: —

      "The sounding cataract
Haunted me like a passion;"

or Byron: —

"I live not in myself,   I become
  Portion of that around me; and to me
  High mountains are a feeling;"

or, above all, Shelley, who drank more
deeply than any at the spring of

          "that sustaining love,
Which, through the web of being blindly wove
By man and beast and earth and air and sea,
Burns bright or dim, as each are mirrors of
The fire for which all thirst."

These poets, each in his own way, threw themselves into nature. They were ready to say with Keats's Uranus, —

" My voice is but the voice of winds and tides."

This feeling was to them, indeed, a religion. Yet in one form or another they all looked " through nature to the God of nature." They felt everywhere the presence of some divine mystery which was open to them in the sweet language of the natural world. Some kind of union with this they sought passionately; and the imperfection of what they were able to attain filled them with sadness, with the delicate melancholy which is an important feature of their work. The religion they cherished was a high and mystical pantheism; only it is essential to bear in mind the profound saying of

N

Goethe, which should never be forgotten when pantheism is in question:
"Everything Spinozistic in poetry
becomes in philosophy Machiavel-
ism." That is to say, the contumely
which universally attaches to pantheism soberly maintained as an intellectual theory is quite out of place in
judging poetry, where the same thing
is present as a desire, not as a creed.

Now, this element of passion, of
intense religious emotion, does not, I
think, belong to our American love of
nature. Even in England there has
been a change in the last half-cen-
tury, a change not enough insisted
on. The difference between the
poetry of Shakspere and that of
Dryden is not greater than the difference between the poetry of Byron and
Shelley and that of Tennyson and
Browning. With the former, intense,

absorbing personal feeling is everything. With the latter, there is a
complete effacement of personality.
Different as are Tennyson and Browning in other respects, in this they are
alike; and though it would be a mis-
take to say that passion is never found
without the intrusion of the poet's
own personality, the lack of passion
is unquestionably the most marked
defect of both these great poets.
Certainly it is the defect in their
rendering of nature. With Tennyson, external nature becomes a mere
means of elaborate ornamentation;
with Browning, it is generally subordinated to the analysis of humanity:
in neither poet have we the peculiar
charm of the generation before.

In America, have we ever had passion in any branch of literature or art?
It must not be forgotten that most of

our great writers have come from Puritan stock; that is, from just that portion of the English race which had the least imagination, the least sensibility; which was the most profoundly penetrated with the moral view of things; which mistrusted most profoundly any self-abandonment, any compromise with the devil. A hundred years hence, the mixture of German, French, Irish blood will have changed all this. The change is going on; but up to this time Puritan rationalism has predominated in the view of nature as in most other things. Take, for instance, Thoreau. No one could be a more devoted observer of nature; no one could record more carefully her subtlest changes, her moods serene or stormy, her infinite variety. His knowledge of natural history was, I suppose, ten times

wider and more accurate than that
of Shelley or Keats. But where in
Thoreau do you find touch or trace
of the passion we have seen in them,
the enthralling, absorbing worship —
call it pantheism, or what you will
— that pants and burns in Keats's
Nightingale or Shelley's West Wind?
Without any assumption of pessimism,
it may be said, as I have hinted
above, that one of the greatest charms
of nature in these poets is the subtle
and inexplicable melancholy that attends her; the vast and fleeting storm
of intangible suggestions and associations that wait on a single simple
sound or odour, and vanish before we
can half imagine what they mean, as
when Obermann writes, "The jonquil
or the jessamine would be enough to
make me say that such as we are we
might sojourn in a better world."

Penetrated with feelings like these, one comes to Thoreau and finds him proclaiming, "The voice of nature is always encouraging."

The truth is, that for Thoreau, as for his master, Emerson, Puritanical stoicism has set up a barrier that cuts him off from half of life. His creed is not a conceited or presumptuous one, — it is too dignified; but it sets the man on a pinnacle of self-satisfaction, which inclines him rather to identify nature with himself than himself with nature. One hears Thoreau constantly saying, "Nature is delightful, delightful to me, Henry Thoreau." He patronizes her. Now, this is inconsistent with passion of any kind. To a man of that temperament the study of nature may be an amusement, even an interesting, absorbing occupation; a religion — never! This is precisely the state of the case, not only with Thoreau, but with most of our American poets, and with the greater number of the men and women who are to-day engaged in ransacking the fields and woods for facts of natural history.

With the love of nature, as with so many other things, the saying is profoundly true, "Unto every one that hath shall be given." We get back only what we give. As a humanizing influence, as teaching patience, tolerance, sympathy, the scientific appreciation of the natural world, the intimate and daily contact with it cannot be overestimated. But to think that these things will ever replace religion or poetry; to believe that the senses of the average man, though backed with all the botanies and ornithologies ever written, will perceive as do those of the poet, will create for themselves the energy and intensity of feeling, the glow of imaginative colour, the throng of associations, which he can call forth in a moment, in the twinkling of an eye, is to be profoundly mistaken.

THE SCHOLAR.

THE true scholar is something quite different from the man of genius or the mere writer. The genius in literature, as in other arts, is intent upon fame, —

" the spur that the clear spirit doth raise."

The keen goad of his inspiration urges him, above all things, to create, not to acquire. Whatever he takes from others is simply assimilated, to be reproduced in a new mould and metal of his own. Some geniuses have, indeed, been scholars, — Dante, Milton, Leopardi, Coleridge, — but by an accident almost in their natures rather than as a result of their creative power.

The writer, on the other hand, the modern man of letters, is generally anything but a scholar. The mass of matter which he pours out upon the world in the shape of magazine articles and essays requires a certain breadth of information, if he is anxious to pursue his calling honestly. But that information is apt to be heterogeneous, gathered from a vast number of books on different subjects, reviewed hastily, and cemented together by a school knowledge of standard authors now and then brushed up and put in order. In fact the specialist is so cut off from the general public, which detests specialties, that a man cannot be thoroughly grounded in one subject and be a popular writer at the same time.

But the true scholar, the real devo-

tee of learning, hardly cares to be a
popular writer. The ephemeral gleam
of fame has rarely charm enough to
lure him from the nook where he has
ensconced himself in the half-lighted
caves of thought. It is difficult for
him to conceal his indifference, or
even contempt, for the *ignobile vulgus*
and the easily excited, easily diverted
curiosity of the magazine world. The
goddess he serves is so austere, so
thickly draped in the dim robes of
mystery, that he half shudders when
one more venturesome among his
colleagues lifts a corner of the veil
and exposes a secret to the vulgar
stare of the uninitiated and unde-
serving.

It will easily be seen that the conditions of American life are not over
favourable to such men as this. Yet
they are to be found here and there,

and cannot be wholly crushed out.
The tradition of their race has per-
sisted unbroken in far more trying
circumstances. It winds down in
labyrinthine obscurity from the starlit
plains of Chaldæa and the first astron-
omers; it passes through the quiet
groves of Academe; it lingers among
the yellow papyri of Alexandria; it
hides its head in the Middle Age
among gray cloisters, poring over
scattered golden relics of Greek wisdom instead of missal or vulgate; it
runs riot through the Renaissance,
mingling together the rites of Pallas,
Bacchus, and Apollo; it walks among
us to-day in men we half honour, half
laugh at,—the treatment which has
fallen to the scholar's lot since there
have been scholars at all. How little
he cares! With his eye turned inward,
"coming upon many ways in the wan-

derings of careful thought," how little
he cares for the ridicule of the world
or its respect!

There is one scholar, however, who
does not hide his head in the nineteenth century — quite the contrary;
and that is the scientist. In some
respects he may be considered the
typical scholar of to-day, and some
people would look upon him as the
natural result of evolution from the
scholar of the past. At any rate, he,
too, is devoured by the passion for
knowledge; only in him it takes form
rather in the study of nature, and man
as an element of nature, than in an
investigation of matters concerning
the human intellect alone. This very
fact of the clearness and sharp definition of the scientist's object takes
something away from the mystery of
his worship. Nature is to him merely

a museum out of order, which he is to arrange and classify, and so often he has an air of patronage, as if it were really very kind of him to do it. Altogether, men of science are too full of the pulse of modern life, too active, too practical to stand well for one's ideal of the scholar. And yet to succeed they must have many of his qualities: his patience, his enthusiasm, his infinite self-sacrifice, his readiness for martyrdom even, in the cause he serves. One has only to read the life of Darwin to be convinced of this.

The scholarship of the past, however, the scholarship which to-day lingers unknown in corners, has little to do with science or the external world. It has an old and worn-out prejudice to the effect that "the proper study of mankind is man," the thoughts of man and the products of his thought. With its eye turned inward this scholarship passes unheeding and indifferent by the loveliness of nature and the mysteries of her existence, in regard to which it is quite content with *a priori* views. It busies itself perhaps with metaphysics, culling wisdom in Plato, or uprooting it in Aristotle and Hegel; or with mathematics, that highest form of intellectual harmony, covering sheet after sheet with endless computation and cabalistic figures; or with philology, tracing the riotous dance of sounds and words from tongue to tongue, or making conjectural emendations in texts that have been thumbed and worn by the brains of thousands long before. But in all these varying forms the basis is the same, an all-absorbing passion for the pursuit of knowledge on the serene heights of thought, a devout abstraction from the cares and interests of active human life, a love of solitary contemplation, which in the intellectual world can only be compared with the rapture of the Brahmin in the spiritual. Who can understand it but the adept, the joy of those solitary midnight hours, when drowsiness has given place to the second and intenser wakefulness, when there is no disturbing sound but the ticking of the clock, and it may be the rumble of a distant train, when it seems as if one could really make books into living persons, and come, oh, so much nearer to them than to the very nearest of one's friends who really live.

This abstraction of the scholar's reacts upon his life everywhere, as is natural. If he has the genuine zeal

of his profession, he looks upon himself as a priest almost, serving a high
and exacting divinity, elevated by that
service above the common interests of
mankind. This lofty office of the
scholar was often dwelt on by Emerson.
"The name of the scholar is taken in
vain," he says. "We who should be
the channel of that unweariable Power
which never sleeps, should give our
diligence no holidays. Other men are
planting and building, baking and
tanning, running and sailing, heaving
and carrying, each that he may peacefully execute the first function by
which all are helped. Shall he play,
while their eyes follow him from far
with reverence, attributing to him the
delving in great fields of thought and
conversing with supernatural allies."
But the true scholar needs no exhor-
tation to the performance of his duty.

o

It is a passion with him. Every diversion, every necessary call of the human relations of life, is a hindrance, to which he submits with vexation and from which he escapes as soon as possible.

It is for this reason that the scholar, if he has his health, is better off unmarried. In the first place, he cannot afford to be rich. The cares and annoyances induced by money are to him abominable and not to be endured. If he accumulates or inherits wealth, he is so apt to become that thing, of the true scholar most hated, — a dilettante. There may have been great scholars who have been rich, but they are rare. Nay, even the distractions of bread-winning — in teaching, for instance — interfere less with these pursuits than the alien and haunting anxieties of wealth.

But marriage to the poor scholar is but another name for misery. Other men do their business during the day away from home, and at night it is their leisure and pleasure to withdraw into the quiet sweetness of family life. But the scholar must either work at home among the thousand disturbances that make consistent application impossible; or, if he goes away from home, half of his energy is taken from him. He is in a strange place, among strange faces, using strange books. And he is haunted all the time by the privations of wife and children at home.

No, the heights of Parnassus are cold and lonely. The intellect is isolating. It is tyrannical. If you give it anything, you must give it all: heart and soul and strength. It will not tolerate half-service.

And then, if one may dare to whisper it in these days, it is better for the scholar not to marry, because women are not scholars and have little or no sympathy with the passion for knowledge pure and simple. This does not apply to men of letters, to whom the sympathy of women in one form or another is almost indispensable. To them women are willing and ready to give it. The artistic side of human nature, the passion for beauty, they can enter into largely. They can enter into the passion for fame, longing for it as enthusiasts, not on their own account, but for those they love. But oh, so rarely, not more than once or twice in a lifetime, does one see a woman who loves thought and study for themselves. In Walter Pater's *Sebastian Van Stork* there is a hint of this: "His mother

expostulated with him on the matter,
— and she suggested filial duty.
'Good mother,' he answered, 'there
are duties toward the intellect also,
which women can but rarely understand."

Nevertheless, human nature must
unbend; even the scholar must have
his recreation and amusement, but
oftentimes it is of a singular nature.
For associates he loves those of his
own kind, of his own specialty, so
that he may share with them little
momentary jottings, may carry into
his diversion the preoccupations of his
graver hours, may season the passing
jest with a line from Horace or a somewhat broad pun from Aristophanes.
And the diversion he seeks seems at
first inconsistent enough with his
tastes. It must be as external, as
unintellectual as possible. He loves

to ramble through the streets with a congenial spirit, to gaze idly into shop windows and read old signs, to criticise women's dress, — everything which attracts the eye and soothes the mind. If he goes to the theatre, he does not want Shakspere or Ibsen. Gilbert and Sullivan suit him better, or even something approaching horse-play. With women it is the same. Blue-stockings and school teachers he abhors. He wants what is young, fresh, full of animal energy and gayety, jests, mockery, of himself, even, if need be. When he comes out of his solitude he wants nothing to remind him of it, nothing external at least, only an occasional reminiscence welling up from his own thoughts.

So, in a manner, the scholar's life is one apart, separate from that of other men. It is perhaps more so in

this our hurried and hurrying American world, but it has always been so.
The scholar is no misanthrope; but
he soon becomes aware that other men
regard him rather with respect than
affection, and he schools himself to it.
They have no interest for him except
as affording him an hour's relaxation,
like some painted, lifeless show, which
makes no impression on his soul.
From the very beginning he feels this.
For the passion for knowledge, for
pure acquisition, is born in him, a
passion so mighty and resistless that
it overwhelms all barriers and acci-
dents of fortune and sweeps him onward in its course whither it will.
Nor does any rebellious instinct
prompt him to oppose it. There is
no deity so imperious, so all-control-
ling. But her force comes from her
charm. Her siren seductiveness has

no limit, no alloy. It enthralls youth, it bewitches age. Still, still she calls, urging the wanderer out into the trackless sea of thought, to which there is no bound, from which there is no return.

The uninitiated, the profane, can appreciate results, but they abhor details. They would gladly discover a new manuscript of Aristotle, or a law of evolution; but they recoil from the endless accumulation of knowledge little by little, the patient observation, the infinite pains. To the scholar the delight is in the means as much as in the end. A happy conjectural reading or the discovery of a new microscopic insect fills him with as much joy as any conclusion to which these things may lead. It is the constant, restless application of mind that he seeks. So the matter worked on be

congenial, he cares but little for the
result achieved. He loves the atmosphere he works in. If it be Greek
texts, he is unconsciously penetrated
with the spirit of his author. Homer
and Sophocles become to him necessary companions. If he is a natural-
ist, even in the minutest research he
is in contact with the vast, loving personality of nature. He cannot be
without her or away from her. Shut
up in cities his life is miserable.

Yes, it is a religion, this worship of
knowledge, — perhaps the last religion
of a certain class of minds, who have
abandoned definite creeds and shut
their lives up in the sweetness of this
one worship, which most of all takes
them out of themselves. For there is
a sweetness in it, an intoxication.
Old Burton, himself a typical scholar,
says of it: "Such is the excellency of

these studies " — he is speaking of mathematics — "that all those ornaments and childish bubbles of wealth are not worthy to be compared to them: *crede mihi*, saith one, *exstingui dulce erit mathematicarum studio;* I could even live and die with such meditations, and take more delight, true content of mind in them, than thou hast in all thy wealth and sport, how rich soever thou art. . . . The like pleasure there is in all other studies, to such as are truly addicted to them: *ea suavitas* (one holds) *ut, cum quis ea degustaverit, quasi poculis Circeis captus, non possit umquam ab iis divelli;* the like sweetness, which, as Circe's cup, bewitcheth a student, he cannot leave off, as well may witness those many laborious hours, days and nights spent in the voluminous treatises written by them; the same content."

As with all other religions, there are
some devotees of this also, who are
ready for martyrdom, the martyrdom
of poverty, of hunger, of nakedness,
of scorn, contempt, and contumely,
the martyrdom of sickness and a lingering death, which attends, alas, too
surely, upon the neglect of the material for the spiritual, of the body for
the mind. Let me quote once more
from a contemporary of Burton, himself also a robust though wayward
scholar, the great and too much neglected Ben Jonson: "I know no disease of the soul but ignorance; not
of the arts and sciences, but of itself;
yet relating to these it is a pernicious
evil, the darkener of man's life, the
disturber of his reason, and common
confounder of truth; with which a
man goes groping in the dark no
otherwise than as if he were blind.

Great understandings are most racked and troubled with it; nay, sometimes they will rather choose to die than not to know the things they study for." How many have so died and are so dying, tortured by the fierce and unquenchable desire to attain truth, so that they cannot for a moment rest or linger by the way, but still press unremittingly, unflaggingly onward, till the torch that has been burning more and more brightly is extinguished forever in the chill dampness of the grave.

Yet one hears people say that the scholar is selfish! Those who bring this charge are as often as not men of business, politicians, pushing and active in practical life, men whose whole souls are absorbed in gratifying their ambition or their greed, whose interests do, indeed, bring them in contact with other human beings, but

who do not hesitate to tread those
human beings under their feet like
ants, if their ambition or their greed
demand it. If it be selfish to follow
with entire devotion the instincts of
one's nature, when those instincts do
not trespass on the rights of others,
the scholar is selfish. Nor can it
be denied that he pursues his studies
much more for his own gratification
than for any useful consequences they
may have to the world at large. At
the same time, they do have such consequences often, and when they do
not, there is an indirect influence
shed by such a life of austere thought
and occupation with the things of the
spirit, which, burning like a quiet,
pale light, pours a ray of pure sweetness on the world. The scholar is
not a philanthropist. He generally
cares little for charities, sometimes

not very much for churches; but the example of his high self-abandonment to an ideal is worth the stir of a dozen busybodies who seek to exalt themselves by the show of benefiting others.

The scholar is not selfish, but he is self-absorbed. And here we begin to lay our finger on his weakness. His whole energy and vitality is given to climbing the snowy sides of this high, cold mount of knowledge, and when he stands on the summit he is indeed isolated and alone. The loveliness, the charm of human companionship, have faded away from him. The natural affections have lost their power. The heart-beat of passion has ceased, and given place to thought at once feverish and cold. While the fever lasts he needs nothing, asks for nothing but the object of his enthusiasm. But the chill comes, and there are times when his brain is ready to burst in that vacuum of silence and the grave. This has always been the case with those who have followed a life of study; but it is even more the case to-day than ever before. Up to this century, or the last, the scholar's province was universal knowledge. He had entered a fraternity of which all the members were bound together by the common service and could meet on a common ground. Now the scholar must choose between two courses: either he attempts all knowledge and becomes a superficial dilettante; or he shuts himself up in one cavernous specialty, and the further he wanders in it the more he is excluded from cheerful day and the community of men. This evil is a terrible one and is naturally on the

increase. On the one hand, all
sciences are so interdependent,
"mutually folded in each others'
orb," that one cannot be raised
securely save on the firm foundation
of all the others. On the other hand,
who can be a master even of the rudi-
ments of all? Thus the biologist
argues incorrectly from lack of knowledge of metaphysics, and the meta-
physician errs from his profound
ignorance of biology and his haughty
contempt for it.

It is these cross purposes in the
world which at times do, indeed,
make the scholar desperate. In his
moments of zeal and hope he pushes
on without looking behind him. What
does he care, if he can only gain one
step in advance, wrest one scrap more
from the close-locked fingers of Truth?
What does he care for love or sym-

pathy, if he can perform the task he
has set before him and satisfy himself? But the inevitable pause comes,
with its gray discouragement. Of what
use is it? How little way can the
search-light of thought dive into the
impenetrable gulf of the unknown, yet
even for that little way it is a guide so
frail and so infirm! Why follow it?
Why leave on one side the real goods
of life — riches, quiet, ease, love,
friends, content — only to wear away
one's soul in the pursuit of an empty
phantom, unseizable, intangible, unprofitable? And he recalls the old,
old words of the Preacher: "Of making many books there is no end; and
much study is a weariness of the
flesh."

Yet, after all, he goes on his way
and fulfils his destiny, sometimes
with hope again and confidence in

P

himself, sometimes indifferent, sometimes with vast scorn for the futility of knowledge and the mockery of life. He goes on, on still, utterly unable to resist the overmastering intellect, which always craves and hungers after more, in the wild desire to get beyond the limits of this earthly body, to enfranchise, to depersonalize, and so to eternalize itself.

www.ingramcontent.com/pod-product-compliance
Lightning Source LLC
Chambersburg PA
CBHW030734280326
41926CB00086B/1517